THIS BOOK BELONGS TO:

THE INTERNET BELONGS TO:

THIS DEVICE COMPLIES WITH FCC RULE PART 15 OPERATION IS SUBJECT TO THE FOLLOWING TWO CONDITIONS (1) THIS DEVICE MAY CAUSE HARMFUL INTERFERENCE AND (2) THIS DEVICE MUST ACCEPT ANY INTERFERENCE THAT MAY BE RECEIVED INCLUDING INTERFERENCE THAT MAY CAUSE UNDESIRED OPERATION.

SERIAL NUMBER: A1   1013057

~~Tim Berners-Lee (age 56½)~~

~~Bill Gates~~

~~Steve Jobs~~

Sergey Brin and Larry Page

Proudly published by Snowbooks in 2011 Copyright © 2011 Will Hogan
Will Hogan asserts the moral right to be identified as the author of this work. All rights reserved.
Snowbooks Ltd. email: info@snowbooks.com www.snowbooks.com
British Library Cataloguing in Publication Data A catalogue record for this book is available from the British Library.
ISBN 9781906727963

CONTENTS

04 GETTING STARTED
- 006> How To Set Up This Book
- 007> How To Use This Book
- 008> Terms & Conditions
- 009> Verification Code
- 010> Reminder Questions
- 011> Disclaimer
- 012> Logging In Level And Flow Chart

14 WHAT IS THE INTERNET?
- 016> Conceptual Scissors
- 017> Ted Stevens
- 018> Timeline
- 021> Place In History: Word Cloud
- 022> Internet Entrepreneur The Board Game

24 NEED TO KNOW
- 026> Elastic Broadband
- 028> Central Unit Of New Technology
- 029> C.U.N.T. Psychometric Test
- 030> Did You Know: GTA
- 031> Jobs Killed By The Internet
- 032> The Wong Maze
- 033> Jobs Created By The Internet
- 034> Internet Ailments
- 036> Did You Know: Test Card
- 037> Moments Killed By The Internet

38 THE INTERNET AND US
- 040> Internet History By Class
- 042> Internet Usage By Country
- 044> Internet Language
- 046> Most Embarrassing Subject Lines
- 047> Kimjongle
- 048> V.S.F.W
- 049> What To Do If The Internet Goes Down
- 050> Now That's What I Call Street View

52 PRACTICAL INTERNET USER
- 054> Make Your Own Youtube Hit!
- 056> Amazon Bullshitting
- 057> Freshly Released Killers Looking For Love
- 058> Email Experiments
- 059> Google Location Arrow
- 060> Onanists Web Planner
- 061> Play Arrow
- 062> Puzzles 'N' Games
- 063> Spinning Web Planner

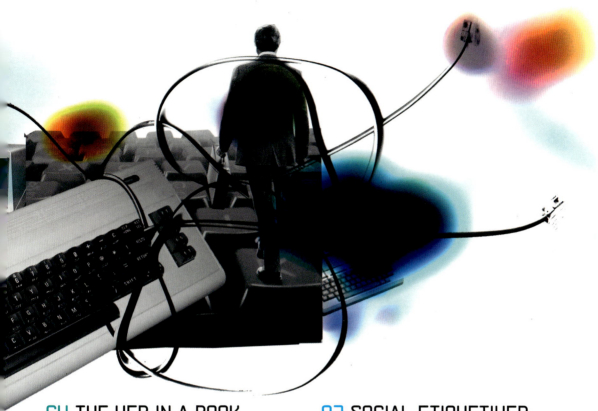

64 THE WEB IN A BOOK
- 066> Nigeria Advert
- 067> Did You Know: Ascii Grot
- 068> Get Creative With Ascii
- 069> Things Google Can't Find
- 070> Error 404
- 071> Rebranding The Web
- 072> Travel With Bovine Air
- 073> Rip Advisor
- 074> Samuel Pepy's Blog
- 075> Greatest Rick Roll's In History Part 1
- 076> Dystopian Dad
- 077> Greatest Rick Roll's In History Part 2
- 078> Conspiracy Theories
- 079> Greatest Rick Roll's In History Part 3
- 080> E-Bay Gum
- 081> Money For Naming Clouds
- 082> Oligarchs Required
- 084> Customers Also Bought
- 085> Naive-Bay
- 086> Memo From Elastic Broadband
- 087> Farcebook
- 088> Voucher Cod
- 089> Take A Break – Google Made Me Vain
- 090> Emotional Bay
- 091> De-Motivational Commemorative Plates

92 SOCIAL ETIQUETIWEB
- 094> Get In With Ryan Birch
- 096> Twitching With Twitter
- 098> Obsolete Inconsequentials From Your Past Re-United
- 099> Build Your Profile To Impress Inconsequentials
- 100> Social Networking
- 101> Social Notworking

102 LOGGING OFF
- 104> 80'S Badges
- 105> Millennium Bug
- 106> Everything's Taken.Com
- 107> Page Not Found
- 108> Meme
- 110> Index
- 112> Credits

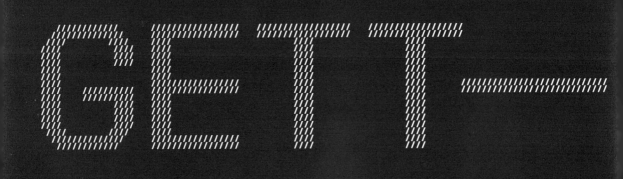

</004/Getting Started>

01

ING START- ED

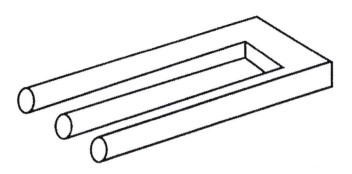

HOW TO SET UP THIS BOOK

Detailed instructions of how, exactly, to use this book are featured to your eyeball's immediate right, here.

Before the *How to Use this Book* page is mentally digested, it may be a pertinent moment to connect the enclosed MIND SPORK™ - as pictured above.

Without the MIND SPORK™, conceptual interface with the contents of the book may prove troublesome, if not mildly disappointing.

If you're still in the bookshop, it may be worth lowering yourself to an all fours position – if not already – and scuttle around looking for the fallen component, possible giving yourself some static frottage in the process. If you've received this book after a rash purchase from an online retailer, please shake the packaging before holding arms aloft and shouting to an unseen power. You may then send a volley of angry emails to the sender with 'Like New' in ironic commas as described some eight words prior. At the very least demand your P&P cost back or simply repeat the cycle by immediately putting the book up for sale on said online retailer, thus completing the online psycho-karmic loop.

Alternatively, if this vital component is missing, you can send off for full detailed instructions of how to make your own for £9.99 plus postage. There's also parts 2,3,4,7B and 21Y which when complete, build into a fully working model of futility.

PO BOX 90210666
Far Away

If your MIND SPORK™ isn't attached here, please ask the shifty-faced Bookseller/Postal/ Charity Shop employee.

HOW TO USE THIS BOOK

Our patented interactive navigation system lets you scroll forward and backwards with ease through this Annual. Simply moisten forefinger and thumb, grip the physical paper dimension where detailed and pull towards the left slowly, until gravity affects the trajectory of the 'Page' and it autonomously lowers its mass onto the left hand side. You can now simply repeat the above motion to scroll through the contents of the Annual. For those having difficulty with the conceptual ramifications and to encourage repeat use, try to imagine operating a slightly more tactile iPad app but with the added hygiene bonus of absorbing the surface germ disco on your fingertips.

Whilst focusing on a chosen page and a picture or portion of textual interest, do NOT try and manipulate forefinger and thumb apart on the page in the hope of making the picture bigger – this will result in creasing of the interface, an irreparable smudge and/or a potential finger cramp.

To quickly find the subject you're interested in, why not use our unique patented search engine which you'll find located towards the back of the book entitled 'Index'.

Read carefully: this book employs technology on the bleeding, bleeping crest of the technology wave, utilising the very apex of modern technological thinking available today.*

*Only applies only to lost tribes and forgotten wizened Japanese soldiers who still think there's a war on somewhere in the Pacific.

TERMS AND CONDITIONS

Terms and conditions of use agreement
Version date: 30.08.11

Please read this carefully, as it's in a barely legible gray and may patronize profusely. This terms and conditions of use agreement ("Agreement") applies to the ("the") book ("Book") as defined herein, forthwith and forevermore is owned by the author and is legally binding in a court of law so help you L Ron Hubbard. By merely by rolling an eyeball across this very page (as defined in a definition, definitely somewhere) you are accessing this Book you are agreeing to the terms and conditions that appear below. If you have any comments or questions please don't bother us lawyer types, we're probably out having a coffee, or simply just basking in the afterglow of billing someone a couple of hundred quid for a couple of sentences.

It is hitherto exemplified that the first party (being of us) and the party to the second party (which partakes to you), should, unless otherwise engaged, be the soul and sole holder of any rights or wherefores what so ever of the said parties. That undertaken and needs be legally insomuch as for the said parties that anyone who disregards the previous and possibly future paragraphs can expect the full punishment of the law as clarified in cases 'Smith verses Ally Mcbeal' and 'Pontly, Pontly and Pontly'. whereby the aforementioned were mentioned in fores and not thirds as previously mentioned. Should any confusion arise from the said documents, further documents may be obtained but only if reference to the documents is referenced. No documents can be submitted however, unless the correct documentation is documented.

Furthermore and thrice onwards, all monies spent on said book are the true and rightful ownership of the two - six said parties that own that, this and anything else they can think of. Good god it's difficult to explain to someone like you but anyway, so to clarify, by reading the previous statement you have entered into a legally and binding contract of corpus, corpus and dumpty dum, which allows the total and complete retrieval of all goods and proxy belonging to the said parties that you do or might leave or not. That said we withhold the right to refuse any of those remains or chattels on the basis that they might be rubbish and not fit for our consumption. However we still might just take them because we can, so there and don't forget it, as you have agreed to it which was your fault in the first place.

In the extremely unlikely scenario that you are still reading this I will now just subtly mention the fact that agreeing to this agreement means we own you, all future you and any possible clones of said you. We also own your clothes, bank accounts and wife, ex wife and wife's undergarments. We might also pop round on every second Tuesday depending on how we feel that day.

Lastly but not necessarily, we the afore mentioned hold not now or ever any relations or responsibility for the contents of this or any other book, we know or don't know about and cannot be held accountable for the quality or goods of said party private or otherwise.

VERIFICATION CODE

Enter the following sequence of words:

Please enter the textual kaleidoscope from the image below by tilting your head, squinting and using sheer bloody guesswork. The letters are not case sensitive, nor wheat intolerant. If not sufficiently baffled, please press 'Sound'. Our guest synthesised voice this week is Kim Jong - il.

1sth1snN0y1nge-nuff?

Enter the letters as they are shown above. It's us against the capitalist computers at the end of the day, comrade.

Email crosseyes2@wtf.com

Password DaytimeSherry

By entering your personal email address, you can be kept up to date with news, events and the latest African coup and subsequent unclaimed currency.

PERSONAL REMINDER QUESTION:

01 Name of first pet

02 Reg number of car that dispatched pet

03 Name of relative that buried pet while you were on school trip

VERY PERSONAL REMINDER QUESTION:

04 Your age

05 Your real age

06 Age at which your first PE teacher made you do sport in your underwear

07 Number of peers laughing at the spectacle

INSECURITY QUESTION:

08 Mother's maiden name?

09 Mother's last boyfriend prior to wedlock?

10 Mother's little soldier?

11 Mother's ruin?

12 Mother I'd like to go and play now?

13 Mother it's cold in the cellar?

'Memory space' - for noting any other instances of personal trauma:

`</010/Getting Started>`

DISCLAIMER:
THIS IS NOT A WEBSITE

No book about the World Wide Web would be complete without a cynical derivative online cash-in. Although the website of the book, rather than the book of the website can be found at www.theInternetstheannual.com this is definitely the Book.

On the website, you'll find little nibbles to accompany the book's more fulfilling nuggets.

If you haven't bought the book, additional online material is available on all pages where you see the Tight Fisted symbol as depicted here:

Glad that's cleared up.

Before using the Annual, it's helpful to identify your user level*

*If you're not sure of your user level, please refer to our flow chart:

Start
Puzzled by that plastic rectangle with the piece of glass attached and those non-wool-based threads hanging out of it? Confused about where the Ethelnet goes? Mind go all fuzzy when grandchildren talk really slowly about plugging the thingaport into the thingaboxem?

No
You confidently pronounce WiFi as 'whiffy', are in awe of 'techies' as defined by people punching the correct digits into a mobile phone and gawp at people using a laptop in Starbucks, continually waving your hand in thin air around the laptop as if trying to dislodge some unseen wire.

No
You know how to upload a picture of you on a jet ski, you're aware of the possible permanent retina scarring implications of typing innocuous words into search engine's images with the safe filter off, know that Stephen Fry was stuck in a lift and can respond to an email without being sold Rohypno-Slim.

Yes
Pensioner

Now go and have a nice cup of tea and a sit down, you'll have no idea what this book's harping on about, but look at the nice pictures anyway.

Yes
Novice

Smoke and mirrors I shouldn't wonder...as for the future of it, look what happened to video cassettes etc. Go steady – perhaps digest a page a week after you've stopped shouting at aeroplanes.

Yes
Normal

I do, just about...that's reassuring. Read on.

Please Indicate:
Pensioner   ( )
Novice   ( )
Normal   ( )
Born post 1990   ( )
Aspergers Spectrum   ( )
Geek   ( )
Stephen Hawkings   ( )
Online Gamer   ( )

Yes Aspergers

May find tone illogical, so go steady.

Yes Stephen Hawking

You're Stephen Hawking, hear you modulate.

And...
Know WLTM from LOL and ROFL, can reconfigure Twitter updates across iPad, mypod, mypig, mobile and the toaster filled with poptarts, upload, download, cross sync, cross hatch whilst expounding how good it was in 1992 whilst googling the 80's and have a thirteen second attention sp..

And...
Know how to re-arrange the previous text in code. And your hair configuration is making me irrationally angry.

And...
Can also do handbrake turns in the living room and deduce mathematically the value of quantum entanglement in determining when, exactly, to buy on eBay.

Yes Born Post 1990

Anyone born post 1990. Some references may be lost but the temporal and non-sequential subjects should align with your genetically hardwired ADHD.

No Geek

No about the hair, but understand the last questions, and can re-arrange this text into binary and Klingon. You have already avoided reading further.

Not Interested Online Gamer

I mainly spend waking hours fighting virtual platoons and virtually communicate with armies and other people without sense of time, space, or personal hygiene and shouting at an electronic box at 4 in the morning.

Illustration: Adrian Dutt

</014/What is the Internet>

02

WHAT IS
NET?

THE CONCEPTUAL SCISSORS

Unless you've been living under a rock, are Sir Cliff Richard or signed up to Talk Talk, you won't have failed to notice the immense sociological redefining of inter populace consciousness - or sheer kerfuffle - that the Internet has created.

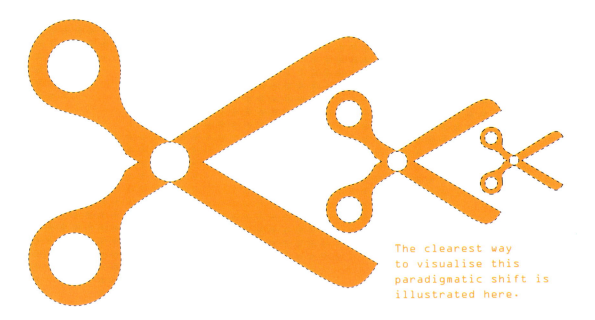

The clearest way to visualise this paradigmatic shift is illustrated here.

Here we can clearly see that it's really difficult to explain: rather like these virtual set of soon-to-be-cut-out-but-not-cut-out-yet scissors which can be imagined cutting out something virtual. To put it another way: in time and space terms, the Internet could theoretically fit into a gap in your keyboard's keys – sitting between the biscuit crumbs and the Legionnaires-inducing bacteria, or spread to fill something larger, like eternity, or within the hold time when calling your Internet provider with a problem. It's an entity not unlike the idea of an infinite number of really self-conscious monkeys typing away at an infinite number of iPads in the largest Starbucks in the universe.

For those that haven't used the Internet, it's like being connected to a giant all-seeing benevolently smiling overlord that's entirely fuelled on our waking hours, our days, our months and our years to power itself. It makes us all 'experts', settles disputes, raises questions, befriends us, comforts us, stimulates us, connects us to the similarly befuddled heads across the planet, all the while making us increasingly bovine as it goes, and something that will eventually destroy us all when it achieves full sentience – estimated to happen in or around 2014.

As for the practicalities - now that's a proposition which can only be answered by an expert.

So over to this transcription from the apparently immortal Senator Ted Stevens.

Puzzled by the machinations of the Internet?
Let this transcription of Senator Ted Stevens make things clear:

"Ten of them streaming across that Internet and what happens to your own personal Internet?

I just the other day got an Internet was sent by my staff at 10 o'clock in the morning on Friday and I just got it yesterday. Why?

Because it got tangled up with all these things going on the Internet commercially.

They want to deliver vast amounts of information over the Internet. And again, the Internet is not something you just dump something on. It's not a truck. It's a series of tubes.

And if you don't understand those tubes can be filled and if they are filled, when you put your message in, it gets in line and it's going to be delayed by anyone that puts into that tube enormous amounts of material, enormous amounts of material."

The Internet didn't just appear like some cosmic Justin Bieber. It took these technology milestones to enable the Internet to be the defining technology of today:

<1969>
US Military inadvertently develops basis for Internet: 'DARNET'. Set up for research into networks to enable the transmission of disparaging remarks to enemy generals during battle.

<1971>
First Microprocessor developed by Intel – work begins in earnest to find world's most irritating jingle.

<1972>
Allan Alcorn creates the game Pong – the first popular arcade game – to the delight of stoners worldwide.

<1975>
Microsoft founded. Paul Allen and Bill Gates signal complete takeover of the planet by cracking open a new vest and a celebratory jar of Horlicks.

<1976>
Apple Computer Inc formed by Steve Jobs and Steve Wozniak. Flares turn pinstripe as corporate assault looms.

<1977>
The two Steves signal a threat to Microsoft's world takeover and Bill Gates' Horlicks is returned to cupboard. Vest stays on.

<1978>
The year that saw Texas instruments release Speak and Spell – devised for interplanetary communication – as featured in the longest infomercial in the world – the film E.T.

<1979>
Apple launches the i-Wurlizter which unfortunately flopped due to users being crushed to death.

The i78 only played 78's in Shellac. Orders could be placed and your chosen track would arrive within 6 – 8 weeks.

Sinclair launches first computer, launches the unsuccessful predecessor to the ZX79, the Sinclair RANDI.

<1984>
Alan Sugar launches signature C.P.U., the Amstrad Plebian complete with Teasmade and alarm clock with Suralan barking disparaging remarks at 4.30 each morning.

<1985>
False dawn of Artificial Intelligence looms with launch of Teddy Ruxpin.

<1987>
Suralan refuses to use Microsoft Windows 1.0 as he launches his own rival operating system – 'Don-tBsoft - Winda's'.

Illustration: Adrian Dutt

Reading Between the Timelines

60's
True to Hollywood archetypes, and like some exploited alien force of good, the World Wide Web was devised by loveable geeky hippies before the cigar-jawed, jack-booted U.S. military stomped in and pledged to use the web to effect world domination. It was only then the U.S. military realised that the 'World Wide Web' at that point consisted of a rotund caffeinated teenager called Randy communicating in binary to a bearded man called Kenneth.

In what was later dubbed the Paisley Revolution, the flared hippies frustrated the flared nostrils of the U.S. military and reclaimed the web of the late 60's with an initial aim of improving the network of available lentil-based products.

70's
The public became divided over the frictional debate over which symbol should be used to denote the 'at' (@) sign on emails.
Some hinted at an early conspiracy when the '@' sign was declared the eventual winner. Allegations of vote rigging plagued the election as its opinion polled favoured '#' hash sign came in second: perhaps deemed too subversive by the U.S. government and too close to the hippie ethos that the senate was keen to forget.

Meanwhile, a slowly smouldering rivalry between Bill Gates and Steve Jobs almost reached room temperature as one time computer club buddies came to almost dislike each other over the relative merits of coding from a flange portal. Corporate rivalries abound and the free-wheeling, laissez-faire programming of the hippie geek era caved into corporate dictum and the possibility of one of the protagonists buying a girlfriend with the proceeds.

80's
Meanwhile, across the pond, in a considerably smaller and an even less glamorous reflection of the epic battle of Gates and Jobs, the Clive Sinclair vs. Alan Sugar battle commenced. Although Alan Sugar was declared the eventual winner after countering Sinclair's ZX80 with an Amstrad Teas'n'F'n'Faxmade, numerous groundbreaking innovations came and stayed in the garage – the Sinclair C5 eventually crowned as the apex of British ingenuity.

The eighties also saw the birth of the emoticon in part thanks to this battle for technological supremacy as :(were the only two keys that actually worked on Sinclair's ZX80.

90's
Step forward Sir Tim Berners Lee and his invention of putting three W's together. The show off barely breaks stride in his tea and Radio 4 consumption to modestly proclaim the World Wide Web as a free service and at last the Internet has a frame to rest its haunches.

00's
Please see our Internet Boom & Bust Board game on Page 22 for a realistic interactive simulation of the late 90's/ early 00's.

<1988>
Sir Clive Sinclair C5 mark II is launched – an updated version of Sir Clive Sinclair himself, with moveable parts.

<1989>
Updated Clive releases the Sinclair anagram, banned because it irradiated the faces of its users.

<1990>
Tim Berners Lee ('Big Bernie' to his friends) in a moment of inspiration invents forward slashes, modesty and the web.

THE INTERNET'S PLACE IN HISTORY

Just how important is the Internet compared with other technological innovations?

Here we compare inventions and phenomena that define humanity's colourful history and progression from primordial soup to the technology smorgasbord that we consume today. Our anthropological team can now reveal their significance in the apex of diagrammatic endeavour – the Word Cloud.

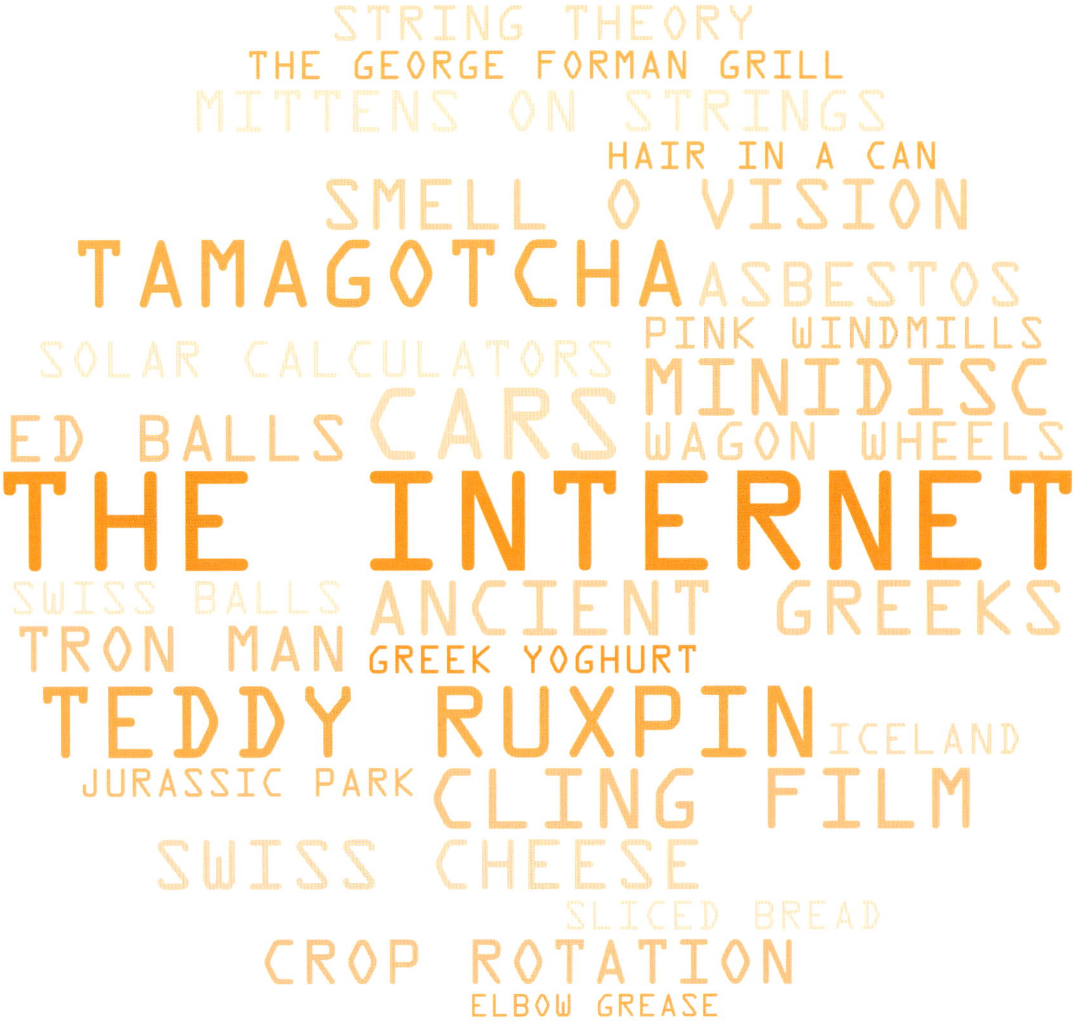

STRING THEORY
THE GEORGE FORMAN GRILL
MITTENS ON STRINGS
HAIR IN A CAN
SMELL O VISION
TAMAGOTCHA ASBESTOS
PINK WINDMILLS
SOLAR CALCULATORS
MINIDISC
ED BALLS CARS
WAGON WHEELS
THE INTERNET
SWISS BALLS ANCIENT GREEKS
TRON MAN GREEK YOGHURT
TEDDY RUXPIN
ICELAND
JURASSIC PARK CLING FILM
SWISS CHEESE
SLICED BREAD
CROP ROTATION
ELBOW GREASE

INTERNET BOOM & BUST: THE BOARD GAME

It's 1999! Make your way as a newly coined Web Designer or self styled Internet Entrepreneur to Internet Boom! Or Internet Bust!

Aim of the Game & Rules:
01 To win, you must land on the 'BOOM! - retire to Quirky Chateau' Square with your accrued cash total BEFORE the opposing players to declare the money in your TOTALISER.
02 You must avoid an ill-judged end which is landing on 'BUST! - see it through to the bitter recriminations with unpaid au pairs' section and lose all accrued wealth in that particular game. In this case, accrued money will not count in your TOTALISER.
03 The winner of the round is the first person to BOOM! And only their accrued cash total will count for that round.
04 Tot up your cash total and those with the highest combined score after 5 rounds is the winner!
05 Any advantages and disadvantages of your chosen character will be revealed upon landing on certain squares.
06 So park up your scooter, pull out your WAP and get going, there's an obscenely rich paper millionaire just waiting to happen!

Illustration: Niebla Roja

Cards and Player Counters:

Consignment of shiny see-through iMacs hasn't arrived for your start-up. A goatey-bearded web Art Director walks out in disgust – go back 4 squares. **Minus 50K**

Whizz round city on a scooter for 3 hours, then your loft style apartment (on the ground floor), order trainers from an obscure Japanese designer…You're wasting time. **Minus 50K**

Some tit in the city wants to know what a website is. Charge him 9 grand for the 9 minute consultation. Move forward 4 spaces. **Gain 9K and a 50K useful gullible contact bonus**

Come up trumps by learning HTML. Move forward 3 squares. **Gain 50K**

Flash course – miss a turn but times your next roll by 2 if you are a Web Designer. **Gain 50K bonus**

Hey, this is 1997! Toast your Gordon Gekko for the 90's attitude – by having a 17 hour lunch break and Chardonnay rub down with potential client – move forward 3 spaces. **Gain 50K**

Some undesirable wants you to buy shares in an online auction site called eBay or some such…send him packing…move forward 1 square. **Minus 100K for foresight miasma**

Beta site gets corrupted by disgruntled programmer and disgusts client – go back 2 if you're an Entrepreneur, forward 3 if you're a Web Designer. **Gain 60K**

Switch roles! It's all the emperor's new clothes in any case! **Gain 50K**

Pre-empt and 'Fix' the fictional millennium bug – move forward two squares and **gain 50 K** for turning the computer on and off again.

Boom! Gain web 200K contract for fashion house – earn **bonus 70K** for wearing turn-ups and stroking chin.

Talking loudly in a bar about a lucrative bleeding edge site and something about an ISDN line earns you a new client. **Gain 50K**

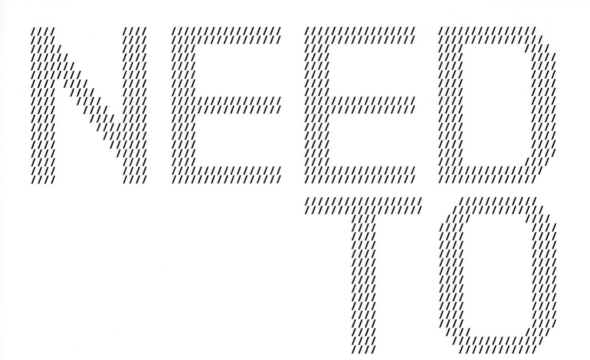

</024/Need to Know>

03
KNOW

ELASTIC BROADBAND

The Internet(s): The Annual has been given exclusive access to a company report from Elastic Broadband.

Here you can see exactly what happens when you sign up to a broadband provider, what you can expect from customer service, and the unique way in which broadband providers function internally to deliver the wonder of the Internet to our screens.

1. Operators here to contact you

2. Operatives here to sell you more products day and night – probably night, to be fair

3. Operators here to ensure payment

4. Operator to take your call in the event of any problem

THE CUSTOMER SERVICE INTERFACE

In the unlikely event of reaching the operator specifically allocated to 'interfacing' problems with your Elastic Broadband service, said caller(s) will be then classified as 'trouble caller(s)' - as defined by person or persons experiencing technical problems of any description.

Let's have a look at the procedure from the perspective of a 'trouble caller'.

01 Your call is taken by our operator in one of our global call centres where he's specially trained to ask you how the weather is in good Sirmadam.
 - You'll be charged the rate set by your service provider which could well be us – with your Elastic Broadband mobile contract – which is fully non-binding with the provision of both kidneys.

02 You'll be directed to a series of 14 multiple choice options. This is where any experience with multiple choice role playing games will be of great assistance. Whilst undertaking the quest, make sure you're wearing the indivisible coat of Herocles to pass the wizards elbow and never pick option 9. Eventually you'll be directed to the Answerphone of Miasma.

03 Here your message is then transcribed through a vocoder into Vietnamese, then back to English via yoghurt pots connected with twine.

04 The message is then handwritten by a drunk strapped to a large gyroscope.

05 Where it's then sealed in concrete and lowered towards the earth's crust.

Illustration: Adrian Dutt

We at the Central Unit of New Technology take your security and privacy very seriously indeed. So seriously, that we look at every keystroke, every search performed, every Facebook update – especially those involving personal trauma or relationship breakdown – keeping these in a special file to cheer us up on rainy days: All for your own safety.

We scrutinise viewing history – in particular those specialist interest sites – noting the times that these sites are visited which strangely coincide with your partner's visit to the supermarket or their work schedule. We look at your purchase habits and transactions, your lax attention to overdrafts, how you eBayed that unwanted birthday present, things you find amusing, where you go on holiday – paying special attention to the pause when considering if you can just add one bag instead of two on that budget airline, how many times you Skype members of your family, the colour of your lucky pants, what you think about your line manager's choice of footwear, and when you cheat at Scrabble: All for your own safety.

We then build a dossier that's kept in quadruplicate for the inevitable introduction of compulsory DNA profiling (we'll swab your keyboard when you're out) which will be sold to the highest bidder or have the data frozen in an underground bunker under a large branch of Tesco and potentially used to recreate your life in the event of assured armageddon: All for your own safety.

Remember, you have nothing to fear but the vast swathes of data you leave behind with each and every electronically documented breathe. **Happy Surfing!**

You can send off for your own badge by enclosing a postal order for £2.99 and a snippet of your own hair

CENTRAL.UNIT.OF.NEW.TECHNOLOGY PSYCHOMETRIC TEST

You're the Winner!...of a randomly selected psycho-evaluation questionnaire by the Central Unit of New Technology!

This is a fun, albeit compulsory set of questions that will help us and importantly you get the most of the Internet. It will not be in any way used to determine your threat level, nor was reported to us by your supermarket loyalty card provider detailing your spending habits and the fact you haven't bought bacon or any pork-based variants for a while.

Section 1
Looks at your virtual beliefs.
Section 2
Looks at your general attitudes.

Just for Fun!
Please use this space to tell us about your neighbours and/or associates

Section 1

When online, do you prefer to:
01 Sit.
02 Lie.
03 Stand.
04 Kneel facing Mecca and recite passages of the Koran.

When using an online chat facility, do you use:
01 Facebook.
02 Skype.
03 Windows Messenger.
04 A complex network of functioning and decoy silos re-routed to rogue satellites via the Middle East and Russia.

Which of the following sentences describe your reaction to the phrase *Prince William?*
01 The people's Prince – where do I buy a commemorative tea towel?
02 Good for the underperforming crockery industry.
03 Marrying below his station but she seems nice.
04 Death to the Infidel and the embodiment of Western decadence.

Section 2

What does 'Freedom of Information' mean to you?
01 An idea best left to organisations that can disseminate the information most effectively.
02 I'm perfectly happy in China.
03 What's that?
04 A necessary construct of a functioning democracy.

How would you best describe yourself on an online dating site:
01 I like kittens.
02 I'm sociable.
03 I have a GSOH.
04 As a dangerously unstable loner with access to firearms.

When given a newspaper article questioning the government, I:
01 Listen to the Elton John CD that's fallen out of the paper.
02 Put my lager down squarely on the paper.
03 Report to relevant authorities.
04 Explore the subject to formulate an informed opinion and flag the issue to friends, colleagues and supporting organisation.

```
00   01   02   03   04   05   06   07   08   09   10
|    |    |    |    |    |    |    |    |    |    |
```
On the above scale, please mark down your feelings for Peter Andre. 1 being gross dissatisfaction and 10 being a credible artist who's got his life back on track.

DID YOU KNOW?
Grand Theft Auto first appeared on web screens in 1974

JOBS KILLED BY THE INTERNET

<#12>
BEING AN EXPERT

Being an expert on a given subject could reap plenty of personal rewards. The passing expert could chance by a happily contested office/pub/street discussion and then liberally douse the debate with a fragrantly informed perfume called 'Smug'. Niche subject knowledge like budgie husbandry, or buttress re-alignment in the Greek church – previously the esoteric property of specialist Marshall Cavendish magazine readers – can now be replaced by anybody with a set of fingers, a search engine and a desire to airily affect knowledge. RIP expertise and memory, long live the amateur.

<#57>
BOOK SHOP OWNER

Back in the dark recesses of time, humans had to trudge to cuboid repositories piled with irregular shaped paper rectangles you had to touch, feel and observe in order to process the data within.

Disturbingly, when purchasing this paper data, you would be forced to engage a human in conversation. Instead of using a faceless algorithm, the 'other' human may recommend a book on subjects you may find interesting or by authors you may like, based on obsolete ideas like empathy and social interaction.

You even had to pick the book up, read a random selection and maybe stumble across a great - previously unnoticed - author and realise you wanted a different, more exciting book than you intended to come out with when you entered. Thank goodness that's all stopped.

<#135>
FAKE DVD SALESMAN

Poor Wong used to be able to pay back the lifetime fee on his special travel arrangement from Xiaoping by serving up a few suspect copies of *Pirates of the Caribbean Mandarin edition* outside the Freight Container & Chinaman. Alas, the Internet's ability to facilitate a half-decent downloaded copy of a chosen film has put pay to that. No more drunk purchases of oddly subtitled blockbusters, no more bumbling silhouette of a bloke in the front row getting up for a whizz halfway through your pub purchase of Saving Private Chan. To commemorate we've given Wong his own game (see next page).

Illustration: Adrian Dutt

THE WONG MAZE

The Internet and its confounded downloading facility has put Wong under further pressure to make ends meet, so help the poor chap safely negotiate the Wetherspoon's Maze.

Look out for obstacles! Negotiate your way past the Dog, Non PC compatible Plod, the grumpy regular's Tankard, the Triad's cleaver, the generic pub racist's Reebok Classic and the No DVD Sellers sign.

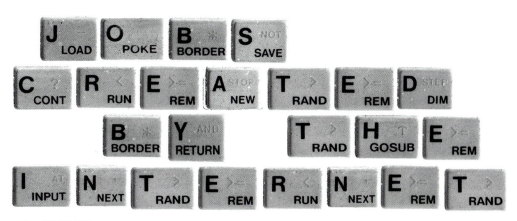

<#565>
PUB QUIZ CHEAT

When not found shouting at Egg Heads or nodding sagely to Only Connect, the pedant could happily take a mid-week stroll to a local pub quiz and gloat over their knowledge like a 33rd degree mason. Unfortunately the partially drunk twit with a phone and Internet connection can carve out a potentially lucrative niche with his charlatan ways.

<#87B> MEME

Or full-time object of ridicule in front of over ten million people.

In the 80s, prawn-sandwiched between the demoralising Saturday TV schedule of before Dynasty and after Game For A Laugh, you had a thing called 'It'll be Alright on the Night', a TV show presented by a man made entirely from the colour grey. Dennis Norden would stand rocking on his heels clutching a clipboard whilst wheezing about outtakes from TV series', films and general programs played in soul bludgeoning succession.

Then came You've Been Framed, a collection of hapless morons caught doing hapless moronic things, like drunkenly falling from garden furniture or rotating around a traffic cone until they stumble through a B&Q fence. The clips would be forever contained to who was watching in that particular country at that particular time. Fast forward to today and we can witness people via various media behaving like morons to the delight and eye-rolling condemnation of the entire planet.

<#39>
CITIZEN NEWSREADER

This. Is. The. News. It looks very important on TV. Smashing dramatic chords open the programme with enough force to cause twinges in Trevor Mcdonald's arthritic left knee and his Earl Grey to rattle in its saucer. Colossal graphics sear the retina of the autocue man with the number 10, and stern-bulleted headlines rain down like a warning from a disgruntled deity – the very adult and professional world of NEWS comes crashing onto screens. And yet citizen reportage is only a blink away and we cut to 'Suzie Smith - aged ten, who has this footage and interview with the Chancellor of the Exchequer via her i-Phone'.

INTERNET AILMENTS

The Internet is fraught with danger. It's not a place for the infirm of body and mind. So look out for these warning signs and avoid the resulting second-degree symptoms.

SOCIAL NETWORKING AILMENTS:

Purported life of Riley being had on a social networking site

First Degree Symptoms Disappointment with reality; reality not being a non-stop conveyor belt of mirth as purported by other profiles.
Second Degree Symptoms Compulsion to photograph social events whilst immediately uploading onto a social networking site to verify the existence of social event whilst supposedly proving the enjoyment of the moment of the social event, thus becoming trapped in a quantum loop.

Being De-friended

First Degree Symptoms Confusion as to whether the initial befriending was imagined and a whole barrage of existential questions – should you re-friend after already being once smite? Forget them forever? Did you de-friend them? Were you ever that close? Should you be getting on with the ironing?
Second Degree Symptoms Indignation leading to an invitation to attend a legal dissolution of your virtual nuptials in a pub car park.

Being in a 'friend request pending' holding tank for over a year

First Degree Symptoms General malaise about not being accepted and inability to look that person in the eye in a real life encounter, with the shuffling awkward knowledge that they know you're waiting for them to accept you on so many levels.
Second Degree Symptoms Paranoia as they've watched you age with your slowly changing profile picture like some virtual Dorian Gray, yet consigned to virtual and quasi-real purgatory.

GENERAL WEB AILMENTS:

Trench Foot from playing online war games for 34 days without relent

First Degree Symptoms Headset purchase for said games – compulsive takeaway ordering in underwear – whilst playing – calling in sick to work – whilst shouting at virtual platoon – ordering colostomy bag to eradicate lost time online.
Second Degree Symptoms When purchasing sequel to said game, crawling across HMV's gaming section claiming conspiratorially to the bemused cashier that you've 'got her six'.

Ebay Bid Usurpment

First Degree Symptoms Wondering if some other twit has put in a higher reserve. Upping your bid to realise the extra 35 pence has made you the highest bidder – suddenly see-sawing from desire to guilt at the prospect of paying too much for a novelty ironing board cover.
Second Degree Symptoms Checking 'normal' sites and finding said item is now considerably cheaper. Ensuing feeling of slowly-rising embarrassment.

Web withdrawal due to being nowhere near a functioning modem

First Degree Symptoms Unease and disconnectedness with (virtual) reality, then manifesting itself in accusations of the locality being in the bloody stone age.
Second Degree Symptoms Tutting and staring into the middle distance – occasional attempts to log on using only the mind: letting the eyeballs swivel in their sockets, medium fashion and reciting your made up 'Tantronic' chanting.

Compulsion to leave disparaging comments about that B & B in Bath on a Trip Advisor website

First Degree Symptoms Pondering naff jam selection at purported 'Best B&B in Bath'. Flashbacks to awkward B&B breakfast silence and the beaky owner's insistence on knowing everything about your weekend.
Second Degree Symptoms Writing review with care not to reveal your true identity in case nosy owner finds you and beats you with a toast rack.

DID YOU KNOW?
This is a copy of the first Internet Test card

MOMENTS KILLED BY THE INTERNET

<#12> ORIGINALITY
Just when you think of something 'amusing', 'original', 'quirky', or 'lucrative', a quick scuttle over to a nearby net portal to tentatively prod your ideas in and...bugger me if some hick in Wisconsin hasn't done it, blogged about it and documented the whole affair on bloody sixteen blogs and a Twitter before you can ask: are there any original thoughts anymore?

<#29> LOTS OF MOMENTS
The black hole of time, space and the true non-event horizon, the Internet is probably the main culprit for the exponentially diminishing attention spans of the planet. Featuring forums arguing the use of a semi-colon to repeated watching of a rotund lad wielding a pole to the strains of the Star Wars theme, we can't resist being sucked in.

<#47> GENERAL WONDER
The wonder of the unknown seems now but a fading historical footnote thanks to the global plugging in to the web. Where once speculation would leave romance in the uncharted, we now have mass coverage where every mind-blowingly mundane status update of friends breakfast, to the knowledge and combined non-opinion of the masses. This is a world where an opinion, an Internet connection and an arsehole are indistinguishable.

<#14> HUMAN FAITH
A writhing mess of information, brain dumping and pithy shorthand :) A tool to exemplify the finer points of human consciousness :(

Realisations caused by the Internet

<#67>
That a large omnipotent search engine is the all seeing overlord. It knows you better than you know yourself. Like a faceless lord Zod, it's merely a matter of time before we're kneeling before its majesty and kissing its ring.

<#128>
Little flash of joy triggered by realising you've 'won' an item on an online auction site – before thinking a little and concluding that you've just in fact 'paid' slightly 'more' for an item than the other person.

</038/The Internet and Us>

04

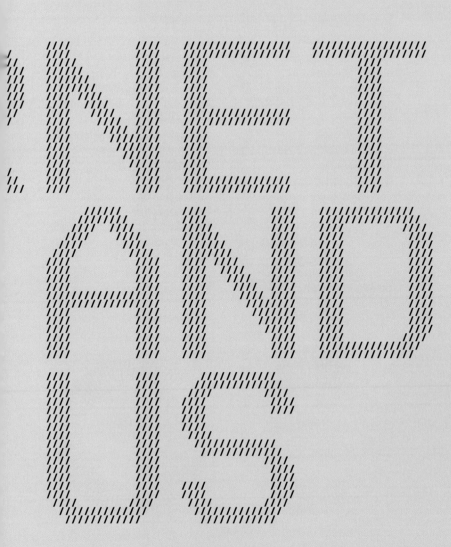

THE NET AND US

INTERNET HISTORY

LOWER

www.argos.co.uk/
loyaltypenoffer
www.preggerstest.com/
inlidlcarpark
www.dwp.gov.uk/
longtermsick-fraud\
beenseenskydiving
www.jeremykyle.co.uk/apply
www.ladbrokes.com/
cockroachracing

Top Searches
02% Removing grease stains from tubigrips
08% Bulk snout deals
45% Facial tattoos for under 9's
45% Can I get preggers if I do it against a wheelie bin?

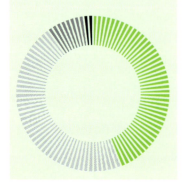

LOWER MIDDLE

www.asda.co.uk/2for1sunny
delight+freadhd
www.sovereignringlandXXXL
.com/saintchristopher-XXL
www.birocompasstattoo.
co.uk/mumstencil
www.newsoftheworld.com/
butlinsforafiver
www.stgeorge4sainting.
com/campaign-signup

Top Searches
10% Is obesity contagious?
25% Removing facial tattoos from under 9's
64% Can I reclaim child benefit from Paddy Power?
01% Does Wetherspoons run a meat raffle?

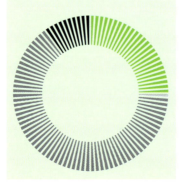

MIDDLE

www.obscurecharitesin
swaziland.com/
conversationalbenefits
www.radio4.co.uk/fanzone
www.sainsburys.co.uk/
jamieoliverpinup/basilpants
www.ofsted.comhomecou
nties/villfiyingteachers
www.rangerover.com/school
run/lollipopladysfromgrill

Top Searches
73% To shush in the cinema?
17% Wanting Hunter Wellies - wrong?
08% Should I tip the John Lewis delivery man?
02% Should I Tudor-clad my Range Rover?

</040/The Internet and Us>

BY CLASS

UPPER MIDDLE

www.ocado.co.uk/
horsehoofdelivery/surrey
www.cravatmonthly.com/
triplewindordaviesknot
www.foxhunting4evr.co.uk
www.tuscanyforum.fr/
winebore
www.dormroomrehab.com/
headbuggerersreunion

Top Searches
02% Camilla Parker-Bowles tattoo on buttock?
08% Can the poor afford opinions?
85% How much is a peerage?
05% Who do I have to fellate to get one?

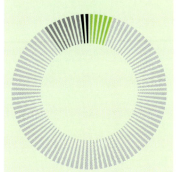

UPPER

www.butlerswives.com/
agamistresses
www.moatcleaner.co.uk/
removalof/expired-househelp
www.blueblood.co.uk/
webbedfeet-benefits
www.capitalpunishment.
com/fanzone
www.blowingholesinanimals
mindingtheirownbusinesson
safari.com/bored

Top Searches
33% Origins of Kate Middleton
17% Is Fois Gras in France?
05% Can I buy the Internet?
45% Is nepotism a disease?

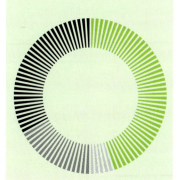

THE INTERNET AROUND THE WORLD

According to our patented unique technology - The Lowest Common Denominator Algorithm™, we can now reveal the top searches and most viewed websites from around the world.

01 Canada
Top websites included www.caringlumberjack.com and www.noimnotamerican.com. Top searches included 'where's my opinion', and 'obtaining larger maple leaf motifs for Canadian travellers'.

02 The U.S.A.
www.reinforcedpavements.com, www.shaftingtheenglishlanguage.com and www.feedersagainstfamine.com came top three in websites and searches included 'where are my feet?', 'do you know Queen Elizabeth Two'? and 'where's Lei – Cester Square'?.

03 South America
Searches involved 'dealing with Munchhausen's syndrome', 'who's president this week?' and 'am I illegal?'

04 Gt Britain
www.weathergripe.co.uk topped the table followed by www.amIhotterthanmybingedrinkinggran.co.uk. Search questions ranged from 'lack of national identity' to 'whether darts is to be recognised as an Olympic discipline in 2012'.

05 The Netherlands
Top ranking webpages are unfortunately unprintable due to EU animal spanking regulations. Next most 'favourited' page was www.***************.c** and www.***********************.*** and banned in six continents.

06 France
The French insouciance firewall prevented our logging of actual websites visited but top French searches involved underarm baguette-holding techniques whilst cycling, beret-wearing at the jauntiest angle, onions, soap avoidance and unique ways of ignoring anyone trying to speak French who's not actually French.

07 Scandinavia
Big hit rates for www.nointernaldialogue.com, top searches included 'sex', 'saunas' and 'having sex whilst building a sauna'.

08 Switzerland
www.ambivalence.com ranked highest and searches included 'who am I'? No other searches or websites were registered by our algorithm due to the national boredom threshold.

09 Germany
Key interest sites were insider guide sites; www.towelsatdawn.com, www.humouryah.com and www.snitzelcraft.com. Prominent searches included 'oom pah pah music downloads' and 'dangers of playing the tuba in naught but Lederhosen'.

10 Italy
www.notsocovertpervert.com came up as the most viewed, followed by the national daily www.misogynistweekly.it and generalist interest site www.whatmedallion.it among an almost completely male demographic*

*We later found that women looking at the Internet or any form of technology more advanced than a rolling pin is prohibited in most Italian regions.

11 Africa
Top websites include www.sevenhabitsofhighlyeffectivespam.com and www.whichwitch.com. Searches included 'missing gold bullion', 'diamonds' and 'a stable economy'.

12 Middle East
Top websites included www.alliedflyingcarpets.com, www.whatcamel.com. and www.justonemorewife.com. Top searches included 'removing sheep blood from carpets'.

13 India
Prolific websites included www.readerscows.com and www.englishphoneetiquette.com. Top searches included 'is there Internet after-sales in the afterlife'.

14 China
www.wisebeardedman.com, www.cookingwithdragonpenis.com, www.cookingwithpets.com top searches includes: 'one of our chihuahuas is missing', 'panda Viagra' and 'will my feet grow back'?

15 Australia
www.beligeranttraveller.com and www.thatsmuchbetterinoz.com rated highest as well as a top search for 'when Rolf Harris will reign as President'.

16 Russia
Most visited sites were www.holidaymenace.com and www.oligarchsneedlovetoo.com.

Top searches involved 're-upholstering Bearskin hat techniques', 'Olga where are my trousers', and 'bear dance-off locations'.

INTERNET LANGUAGE

The language every1's in2!
Take r quiz and test ur knowledge!

VOCABULARY HIERARCHIES

01 'Is a Smoking Fox better than a Hottie?'

02 'I can haz difficulty in later life stringing a sentence together'

03 'A Cougar breaks into Bernard's Crib, do you swot it with a Phish?'

04 'Is Debbie more advanced than a Noob?

05 'A Packet Internet Groper is Chillaxin' with a Cappuccino Cowboy, what do you do next'

06 'Vulcan Nerve Pinch a Nifoc and what happens?'

ACRONYMS

01 CRPTBRN
02 MLKNEESYKES
03 CHZNPNPLLEONSTX
04 JOYRDNGINAMNDEO
05 SOPEONARPE
06 MXNSPX
07 NTHXWRBTSH
08 IKEA

BONUS POINT

OJCTRNVIISDINLN

Answers

01 Yes, Smoking Foxes are further up the Microchin than Hottie's — which are in turn one up from Cougar's but not M.I.L.F's nor the Long Eared L.y.n.x.
02 Correct.
03 Absolutely not. Cougar's are notoriously Cribbins prone and should not be swotted with a Phish. Perhaps initiate a Kirby Death Grip.
04 Debbie's are more advanced than a Noob, but not in the Meat Space otherwise you run the risk of Clusterfunk.
05 Huge pipes.
06 Ctrl Alt Del Mar.

Acronyms

01 Carpet Burn
02 Melanie Sykes
03 Cheese and Pineapple on Sticks
04 Joy Riding in a Mondeo
05 Soap On a Rope
06 Marks & Spencers
07 No Thanks, we're British
08 IKEA

Bonus Point

Oh Jesus Christ, that's really not very appealing infact I'm so disgusted I'm no longer naked

---

</044/The Internet and Us>

KNOW YOUR EMOTICONS

Here's our simple guide to some everyday emoticons

x<|:0/
A morose clown has broken into my home and refuses to get up from the sofa

:-[
Cynical vampire cash-in TV series about to start

(((x⌡x)))
I'm in a Beatles tribute band

<(-_-)>
Another George Lucas franchise imminent

~0-0~
Pensioner offering advice nearby

(0 Y 0)
I can see a Katie Price book signing

C]:{D
Passing Mexican/Spiv stereotype

<x((((><
Have a Christian sing along with me!

{
Spare moustache if you need it

£[ ]
Overpriced coffee?

Vet required

?:[
I've got some Morrissey tickets spare

MOST EMBARRASSING SUBJECT LINES TO FIND IN INBOXES WORLDWIDE

Your Subscription to Chaps in Chaps has expired

Your Amazon order has been delivered: It's a Boy

Margaret Thatcher has accepted your friend request

Karachley's Bank: Thank you for your bank details

Welcome to the President Mugabe Fan Club

Scientology News: Reptile Leaders Special

Jilted.com RE: Effectiveness of Arsenic

Ticketmaster: 2 x Admission to Bennie from Crossroads sings Sinatra

Your completely legitimate £24.99 PHD certificate in Neuroscience is attached

Internet(s): The Annual Factoids!
'Your Keyboard is home to 84 different types of Bacteria — and only 78% contravene EU regulations'

</046/The Internet and Us>

THE NORTH KOREAN SEARCH ENGINE!

Use our specially designed
gateway to the world!*

Kimjongle Search | I'm feeling Oppressed

Congratulations!
You have one of five available search options!
Choose from our drop down menu...

KWPedia

KWPedia. Our chosen webpage this week is how our beloved leader created the espadrille

Shop Online

Shop online from one of two officially mandated dress codes

View Images

View images of North Korea's footballing heroes lifting the annual World Cup

Social Network

Our very own social network – share your thoughts with the country and our network of state-appointed friends.

Camping Adventure

How our camping adventure holidays really help you concentrate on your synchronised beliefs

* Exclamation marks or exclamations of any kind are not permitted after 2pm Monday to Monday.

VSFW

To counter the fact that one in four sites accessed on the web is in fact pornography, The Anti Smut Society has provided a definitive list of images that should be propagated to ethically counter this content – and be the much needed sedative to today's fast moving bombardment of salacious images.

So calm down, stare at a half-finished bowl of Cornflakes, think of Tim Henman, put the kettle on and on no account think unclean thoughts.

Two Birds, One Cup

A Small Kitten in Some Laundry

A Bowl of Fruit

Morning Wood

A Little Dog with a Stick

A Lake with Some Fountains in the Middle

Now that's a lot better. If you do happen to think of any lascivious thoughts after seeing these most un-suggestive images, please seek professional help or mental picture of some discarded tights on a roundabout. In Milton Keynes.

WHAT TO DO IF THE INTERNET GOES DOWN

Despite having no official government mandate regarding what to do in the event of a global internet meltdown, here's our handy guide.

Relax. Everything may be just fine. Even though the non-stop Niagara of information, communication, entertainment and eye-watering smut that you have previously been bathing in has been abruptly turned off, there was a life – albeit an ill-documented and ill-conceived life – prior to the Internet.

Try and recall what life was like prior to the World Wide Web. Resist the futile temptation to summon the now-defunct Google, and instead use your the organ located directly behind the eyes to summon memory. Refer to any books, newspapers or paraphernalia you have from the 1980's for guidance.

At this point it may be worth taking a few moments to stop banging your head against the radiator, rocking and staring in mortal disbelief into the middle distance and contemplating holding a mini wake for your iPad.

After suitable amounts of courage have been summoned, you can try opening your front door approximately 4-6 inches or the angle width it takes to trigger the sleep mechanism of your laptop, to view the world outside.

After 6 or 7 hours have elapsed, try and emerge doe-eyed and blinking into the natural light of day. After a while perhaps try communicating with real people – go easy now, perhaps start by talking to someone through a square frame to resemble a Skype conversation, occasionally pausing mid-sentence for the correct effect. Take care to cover your nose and do not look directly at them – the last thing you need at this stage is sensory overload.

If the lack of Internet is more permanent, try to remember that living 'Off Grid' is very fashionable these days with bearded men and liberal free thinking woman in polygamous marriages.

Illustration: Adrian Dutt

NOW THAT'S WHAT I CALL STREET VIEW

Street View offers a wealth of armchair excitement; it's like touring around your favourite cities as though you've just imbibed some nasty transcendental medication or simply viewing the rich tapestry of the world through a smoke filled milk bottle. The blurred faces just seem to add to the sense of fun. It's perfect for those who may be bored, unstable or planning a robbery. So we've put together a selection that really shows Street View at its very best in 'Now That's What I Call Streetview'.

Street View found this levitating line on New York's 43rd street

Street View is quite comprehensive in its coverage

Spotted - Pope'in out for a pint of milk

This colourful character has been shouting at traffic since 1974

Caught out – this unlucky fellow has been seen coming out of a Lenny Henry gig

Sinner or Winner?

The invasion didn't go unnoticed.

The final frontier? – not if Street View's got anything to say about it.

Victoria Beckham can be just be made out looking scornfully at the queue of this donut emporium.

</052/Practical User>

Our extensive research into the phenomena of YouTube has enabled a definitive formula for you to deliver a failsafe* instantaneous Internet sensation.

Simply pick one of the options listed in each section, obtain the relevant items and film the results – it really is that simple.

So close your eyes, twirl your pen over the page and then stab the paper once in each section to reveal a winning formula!

Pick from the mix and match items on the right!

```
Safety Message: When
bringing the pen down
in a stabbing motion
onto the page, take
care to remove the hand
holding the book open,
as this could cause
injury. If you are
intending to disregard
this safety message, at
least have the decency
to film the event and,
of course, upload.
```

Everyone's a winner, but here's our experts' assessment of possible outcomes and viewer reactions:

The Majority Of Your Selections Were:

01's Your own chatshow
02's Shadenfreude Joy to millions
03's Guest on Jeremy Kyle
04's Offers for your hand in marriage (or failing marriage, just your hand)
05's Ahh...Cute!

Subject:
01 Rabbit
02 Reporter
03 Seagull
04 Cat
05 Rotund Child

Hallucinogenic/ Drug Of Choice:
01 Ketamine
02 Self Importance
03 Miaow Miaow
04 M.S.G.
05 M&S Walnut Whip

Location:
01 Kitchen
02 Vinyard
03 Motorway
04 Wetherspoons car park
05 Your Gran's living room

Background Music:
01 Justin Bieber
02 A medley of agony and embarrassment
03 Lithuanian Speed Folk
04 Fleetwood Mac
05 The Charlstan

Additional Items:
01 Diet Coke
02 Unsympathetic News Anchors
03 Cattle Prod
04 Prophylactic
05 Sugared Almonds

THINGS TO DO ON THE WEB (TTDOTW)
AMAZON BULLSHITTING

Why not post a review or two to help readers and potential purchasers make their mind up?

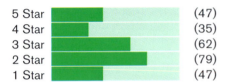

5 Star		(47)
4 Star		(35)
3 Star		(62)
2 Star		(79)
1 Star		(47)

Most Unhelpful Customer Reviews

★★★★★ 'Ubermensch-ken', 22, Dec 2010
Aunty-Christ-ine (Brighton) See all my blackened opinions and Prozac flavoured reviews
Comprehensive look at Nietzsche's god complex within Ken Barlow's seminal years – brilliantly covered in the Corrie Best Bust-Ups DVD. Un-missable for nihilists.

★★★ 'Hello?' 11, Dec, 1987
LionelRichTea (New York) See all my confusing of various artists
Not one of Stevie Wonder's best to be fair, yes it features tracks like Superstition, Living for the City, I Just Called To Say I Love You and Master Blaster, but where, oh where, was Dancing on the Ceiling, Hello, or All Night Long?

★★★★★★★★★★★★★★ recurring. 'Crisp Watching', Feb, 2012 AD
MaxiumusGluteus (Roma) See all my imagined Crisp and Watch based fantasies
Great film, but one for the spotters - if you look closely in the closing scene - the Centurion behind Russell Crowe's Maximus seems to be wearing a calculator watch and eating a bag of crisps (Smokey Bacon?)

★★★★★ out of ★★★★ 'Brucie Bonus' 15, Mar, 2015
By **Joy-Bludegeon (London)** See all my bitter revealing of film and book endings
Outstanding. If you haven't seen this film, you really should: massive twist at the end and in fairness I wouldn't have seen the fact that he sees dead people. Sees. Dead. People. Marvellous stuff.

★★ 'Mechanical' 14, Jun 2011
Draftyvicarage (Home counties) See all my deranged ex - English literature student rantings
Jane Austin's Emma is filled to the brim with bubbling sub-plots depicting class protocols and perfectly framing snob matchmaking Miss Woodhouse as conduit of the romantic ideal and as the consummate former day Amelie. Shame, though, she turned out to have an electric elbow.

FRESHLY RELEASE KILLERS LOOKING FOR LOVE

Why not start up an intimate friendship with a 'lifer' at www.freshlyreleasedkillershungryforlove.com on a friend's behalf?

Why not befriend an inmate? Sending them a letter, a note or just a fingernail in an unmarked envelope can make their seemingly endless stay behind bars that bit more tolerable. Any contribution you can make to enrich their lives with a few well chosen words can be the start of a 'lifer long' friendship as we like to say here.

Please remember though that any break in correspondence could cause offence and possibly the start of a lifetime of stalking and daily threats to use your lungs as slippers.

Select from our two inmates of the week, due for parole in a town near you, very soon:

Lord Bubba and his divine meat rod of justice

Killer Face Cruikshank Mcgraw A.K.A Agnes

Lord Bubba
Member of The Death Rowing Team, Bubba may look harmful enough, but, like his teeth, he has a heart of solid gold. He's 6 feet four and has a lovingly etched picture of David Ike on his forehead. He enjoys quiet walks in the country with strangers – from a discreet distance, of course. Bubba has also been known to be quite outspoken: occasionally wearing his heart, and other people's vital organs, on his sleeve.

Killer Face Cruikshank Mcgraw
Killer Face Cruikshank McGraw A.K.A Agnes to her friends describes herself first and foremost a people person, despite spending much of her time in solitary mastering macramé. These rich tapestries depict her life's trials and tribulations and she's working on a life size model of Mira Hindley in macrame right now.

EMAIL FUN

E-mail's great! It's taken the permutations for misunderstanding to a whole new level as well as the perfect faceless medium for the cowardly to have a moan.

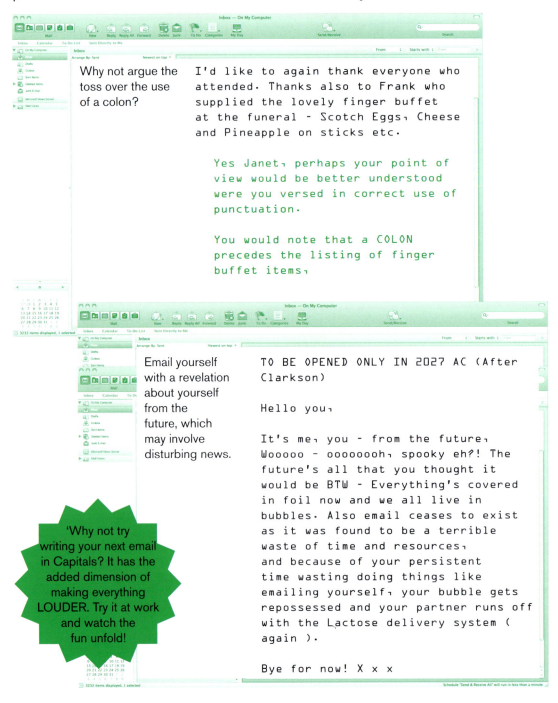

Why not argue the toss over the use of a colon?

I'd like to again thank everyone who attended. Thanks also to Frank who supplied the lovely finger buffet at the funeral - Scotch Eggs, Cheese and Pineapple on sticks etc.

Yes Janet, perhaps your point of view would be better understood were you versed in correct use of punctuation.

You would note that a COLON precedes the listing of finger buffet items,

Email yourself with a revelation about yourself from the future, which may involve disturbing news.

TO BE OPENED ONLY IN 2027 AC (After Clarkson)

Hello you,

It's me, you - from the future, Wooooo - oooooooh, spooky eh?! The future's all that you thought it would be BTW - Everything's covered in foil now and we all live in bubbles. Also email ceases to exist as it was found to be a terrible waste of time and resources, and because of your persistent time wasting doing things like emailing yourself, your bubble gets repossessed and your partner runs off with the Lactose delivery system (again).

Bye for now! X x x

'Why not try writing your next email in Capitals? It has the added dimension of making everything LOUDER. Try it at work and watch the fun unfold!

GOOGLE LOCATION ARROW

Why not make this handy Google Location Arrow – perfect for someone coming round your house for those who may have used Google maps and needs your help.

Simply place the Google Location Arrow proudly in front – or just append straight to the roof of your establishment.

Fully portable (when driving a articulated lorry)

ORNANIST WEB PLANNER

Men. Can't decide what to do on the web? Let the Onanists Web Planner decide - you'll always be guaranteed a satisfactory outcome.

INSTRUCTIONS
With your free hand simply cut closely round the perforated lines around the Spinning Arm Pointer.
01 Affix Spinning Arm Pointer to the centre of the blister board with a pin (not provided).
02 Spin the arm, await to see where it lands and away you go!

For guaranteed fun for one at least one member of the family.

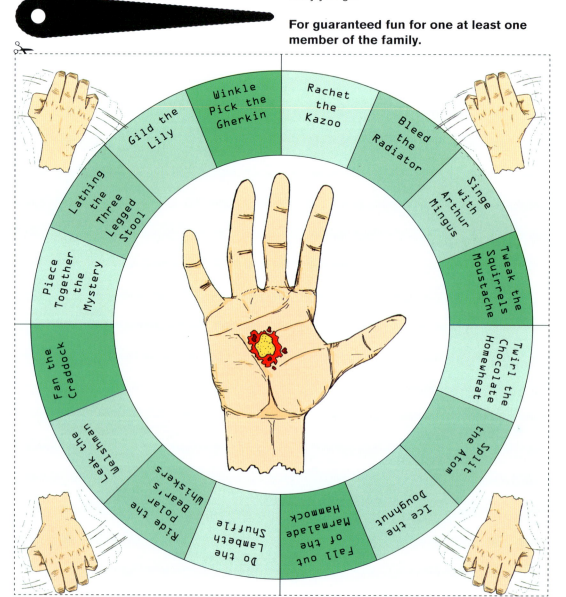

Illustration: Adrian Dutt

GIANT PLAY ARROW

When sending a video of yourself to a friend, simply cut this arrow out and stick on your head and keep perfectly still.

The joke will be on them when the poor saps keep pressing the arrow only to find that the 'Play' button won't work. Try not to titter though! You may choose to or not to reveal that you've got one over on the poor saps before revealing you're not to be trifled with.

01 Cut Out
02 Stick to Forehead
03 Get Camera
04 Align so your Play Arrow is Dead Centre of Shot
05 Keep Still For Duration of Video

PUZZLES 'N'

All you need for this fully interactive fun is this book, a pen, and a gnawing sense of desperation.

The rules are almost straightforward. Find the Tech 'n' Web based word associations listed below. They read horizontally both directions, vertically both directions, diagonally both directions and also in many directions at once. **Alternatively**, in the event of extreme ennui setting in, simply relax your eyeballs as though looking at those early nineties magic eye pictures usually found adoring the walls of Amsterdam cafes and 90's student bedrooms. Concentrate for long enough and you may indeed see the intended portrait of Nelson Mandela.

```
H U B L L O R K C I R R
D S A 4 O 4 R O R R E S
U B N W R I S T S U N Y
O U J H I T A N E H C A
T P A G E E X P I R E D
R Y X M I M W W W M O N
A I C O D E E R R O R O
E Y A N O M M O T I C R
H I B L Z U E P Y D N A
P I L L S M Y P I L L S
Y O E R I M G A U Q W H
I H T G N I O D I M A Y
S T O M Y S E L F W H Y
```

The words contained are listed here as well as others you may choose to find:

Code Error
Quagmire
Www
I.T
Randy
Pillsmypills
Pageexpired
Rickroll
Banjaxcable

Mum
Modem (NL)
Wrists
Iheartu
Mondays
Error404
Hub
Emoticon
Ropey

Why Am I Doing This To Myself Why (NL)
Bonus Words:
Bacon (NL)
Terminate (NL)
Truncheon (NL)

(NL) Denotes Non Linear

</062/Practical User>

GAMES

Need web inspired things to do? Well simply cut the spinning web planner, spin and watch the fun unfold!

01 Learn how to edit a Wikipedia entry - for forty-four seconds before realising it's easier to learn Swahili.
02 Make your own YouTube hit with our definitive guide to web-based stardom.
03 Hack the U.S. Military mainframe, and start a humanity-defining game of noughts and crosses.
04 cle'a]n.e y7'r ke]yb29oa;rd
05 Actually cut out the spinning web planner – we know you're just reading this.
06 Log on to trip advisor and review an imaginary Holiday.
07 Build the first scent-based website.
08 Compose your own Pentium™ style sound – making sure that no matter wherever you are, if you hear your name, you make that sound.

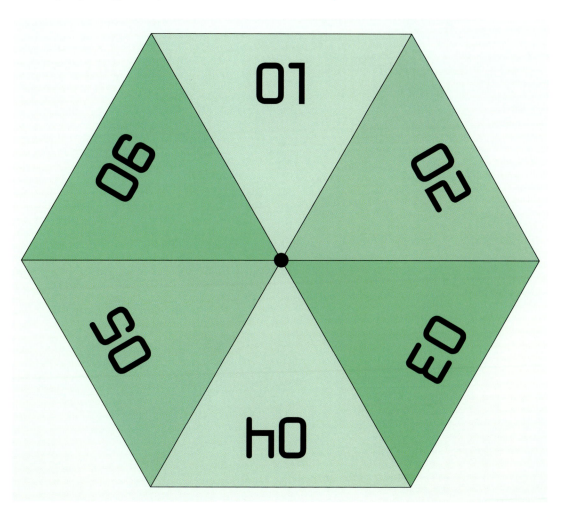

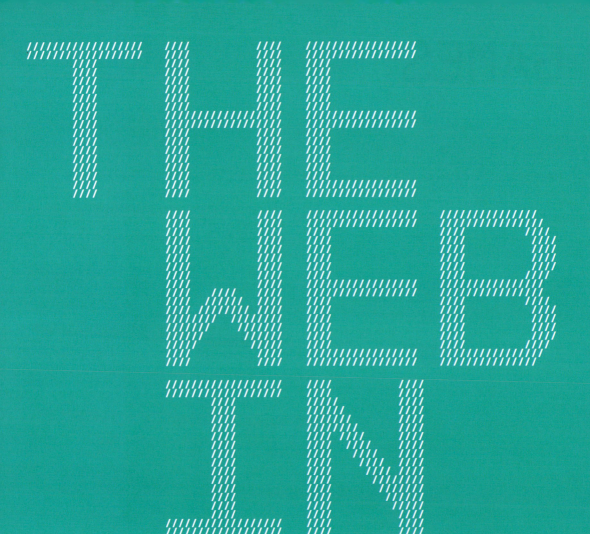

</064/The Web in a Book>

06

A BOOK

DID YOU KNOW?
The first Internet filth caused ruptions...

The rest was met with complete outrage...

GET ASCII CREATIVE!

With our Downloadable* program that lets
the Ascii your own design! Simply and
quickly** cut out individually and get
creating***!

*When we say downloadable we mean use a pair of scissors.
**When we say simply and quickly we mean may take 7-8 hours of hand cramps.
***When we say creating, we mean losing the will to live.

THINGS GOOGLE CAN'T FIND

Our exhaustive research has found just 10 things a large search engine it isn't able to find:

- A decent cup of tea at a British service station
- The Pig from the original 'Now that's what I call music' album
- A repentent banker
- My Nan's medication
- A sober postman
- David Cameron's soul
- Something Katie Price won't do for a show on Living TV
- A sense of self-worth
- John Prescott's feet
- An amusing anecdote from a software programmer

'Since the introduction of Street View, you can see the enormous disparity in paycheques between you and your colleagues by comparing where you each live'

ERROR 404
PAGE HAS CRASHED

The page you were looking for might have been removed, had its name changed or be temporarily on a witness relocation program.

Please try the following:
01 If you typed the page address in the address bar, make sure that it is spelled correctly — try co-ordinating your eyes with your hands and fingers.
02 Open the www.example.com homepage. Not literally 'example.com' and then look for links to the banal/self aggrandising/obscure and probably obscene information you want.
03 Click the Back button to try again, then perhaps forward again — like when you lose your door keys and keep looking in the same place even though you've seen it's not there four times before.

HTTP 404 – File not found

PRESS RELEASE

Rebranding the Internet and the World Wide Web:

We at Tootle, Pootle & Scoodly Bup Bup creative advertising agency will be re-launching the World Wide Web.
Suffering from somewhat of a free thinking ethos, we think there are too many elements that seem to be left untouched by the withered claw of commerce, too many spaces between the lines - so to speak - that simply aren't filled by brain buggering corporate idiom, or the chance to buy a trouser press.

That's why we have a three pronged holistic, systemic, totemic and all round elastic-snapping strategy:

Webucation Because the campaign must start at grass roots level – that's the beginning to you, consumer. We're home to some of the biggest names in infotising and the kind of people who sit in glass offices, making up words whilst playing table football and getting paid an immoral amount of money to wear bright limited edition imported trainers, sneer post-ironically into the middle distance and generally charge the national debt of a small country to make a Powerpoint on panty liners. Where were we? Kids, yes children, are the future, not to mention our safe medium for long term indoctrination.

Weligion Because unless we have a platoon of bleating acolytes for our brands, then our figures won't look as good. Again, that will affect the amount of angular haircuts we can have per head, per annum, our choice of houses in the country and in the worst case scenario, the choice of public school for our children - which research proves has a proportional effect on the amount of marketing jargon and word-bastardising we can produce on a given week. And that's got to bad all round. So we're going to Make Your Modem your Mecca™.

Worality That's the word Morality and Web combined, get it? You as joe public probably thought that's a word tumbling out of Cheryl Cole's maw, when she's trying to sound 'intelligent' and not from some grotty estate. Well that's what you pay us for when you need something sold to the masses of morons we refer to as consumers or 'the public'. And where would we be without the ethics of morality on the web? We'll make sure there's nothing immoral on the whole thing, nothing that may question or be a threat to thoughts outside of our branding guidelines.
Thank you for your co-operation. You really don't have a choice, but we thought it only polite to mention.

BovineAir.com

Tax Details

Priority Boarding Tax 15 Euros
We'll make sure that you're sat in the front of the plane, therefore in the perfect vantage point to watch even more plebeian boarders of the plane look at you with a mixture of envy and quiet indignation that you've got an extra 5 Euros spare.

Arse on Cloth Tax (not optional) 20 Euros
Intend to sit on the plane? This will cover wear and tear on the fabric – and the cattle prod stays sheathed.

Baguette Sans Botchilism Tax 10 Euros (each way)
We'll pick one from the very bottom drawer of the hostess trolley – ensuring a veritable microbe orgy in mock Italian dough.

Burnt Faced Stag Party Tax 10 Euros
We'll sit you directly next to 'Shit Head Shagger' upon failure to tick this box.

Lazy Bastard SMS Tax 5 Euros
We'll send you a text for only ten or twelve times the going rate because you can't be bothered to write down this series of numbers and letters.

BONUS!

Also includes offer of international germ transmitting device and thinly veiled compendium of adverts known as the in-flight 'Magazine'.

Approved Cabin Bag
(Dimensions actual size)

Don't ask us to provide a boarding ticket - you can provide your own as we prefer bits of scrunched up a4. Thinking about it, you've just incurred 40 Euros charge for asking.

RIP Advisor

Club 1830 - party like the Victorians! Games include: What the porter saw. Suppressed violence and fishing excursion - Don't spare the Rod

Swinger's beach - chuck the keys to your pedaloe and let the fun begin! Not recommended for anyone easily offended, or any sense of self worth. 'The Animation team will be sure to ogle your partner and make inappropriate comments whilst mithering you every other minute to take part in tonight's adults-only game of Swingo.'

REVIEWS:

Sort by Indifference / Vitriol

"Musn't Grumble" ★★★★
Mrs. Corby, Middle England, Middle Englandshire, Surrey upon Tescos.
The minibar only contained a solitary bag of chocolate nuts with the word chocolate crudely crossed out in biro. Invariably the nuts seemed to have had the chocolate methodically chewed off each one and carefully replaced. The air conditioning was just one of the porters standing behind a 2 foot sq of grill blowing for several minutes at a time – before needing to catch his breath and chew more mints. The room itself was just a square of earth, marked out with bent tent pegs – needless to say we could hear the kitchen staff moaning about the fact that Derek's sarong was a size too small. Still, weather was very clement, which did incur a surcharge.

"Food not fit for a foreigner" ★
Phillis Stein, Little Nous, UK
Food tasted just horrible and foreign. At one point, I ate un-battered fish served with Lemon! The chips I ordered didn't even have curry sauce on AND most bizarrely I was handed a square of cotton material to accompany the meal (Napkin?). If it wasn't for the suitcase full of beans, I wouldn't be here now writing this! Steer clear! Also...some of the waiters only had English as a SECOND language.

"Awful, Awful, Awful - Will Return" ★★★★★
Riley Lachrymose, Black Country, Gaping Void
I rarely get a chance to spend two solid weeks complaining, so it was with great pleasure that I ended up at the Paco Rabanne. It's essentially given me something to fill the gaping void in my life called pleasure and I now have this awful experience to regale whenever the word 'holiday' comes up in public forevermore. Thank you!

"Gap? Yah" ★★★★★
L Jeraboam, Buttery knob upon Tweed, Rule Britannia
After spending 20k on two weeks' pygmy sniffing adventure in Patagonia, which did actually involve lying in a mudpit for nine days, and sustaining myself only with my own hair, I wanted something just that bit more edgy. And this place did not disappoint.

Samuel Pepys Blog
E-Gads about town

14 April, 2011
Comments 0
Add Your Comment Here
Tags: Coffee / Relations

At noon to the Coffee-house, where excellent forum discourse with meatandpotatohead435, who proposed it as a thing that is truly questionable, whether there really be any difference between mobile device connectivity speeds with wlan and the incumbent mobile phone provider.

   I came home to supper and to bed. It was a sad sight, me thunk, to-day to see Lord Peters coming out of the House fall out with his lady (from whom he is parted) about this ghastly Facebook business; saying that she disgraced him. But she hath been a handsome woman, and is, it seems, not only a lewd woman, but very high-spirited as the Barbados '10 album lays testament.

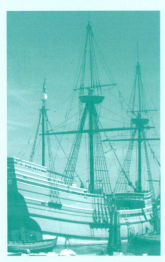

16 July, 2011
Comments 12
Add Your Comment Here
Tags: Electronic Etchings

Up and to my office, where busy, and by and by comes Sir W. Digby and old Mr. Bond in order to the resolving me some questions about electronic etchings of masts and their proportions, but he could say little to me to my satisfaction, and so I held him not long but parted and forwarded the subject of conjecture entitled NSFW.

   I was at it to-night, but durst not stay long at it, for *Farmville* is the blight of our times. I being come to have a great pain and water in my eyes after LCD-light.

```
Gout247: Masts! Lomlwpfcods! ( Laughing out moderately loud whilst
politely following conventions of dignified society )
QuakerQuaker$$: Fascinating. What was the length and girth of the
largest?
DukeofpOrk: oi Quakers. He's not talkin bout actual masts you (0)(0)
QuakerQuaker$$: I'm aware @DukeofpOrk !!! of that!
DukeofpOrk: You're awarin' lady's undergarments more like...
COMMENT WAS REMOVED BY THE VERY MODERATE MODERATOR
```

GREATEST RICK ROLLS IN HISTORY 01

From: George Bush

To: Tony Blair
CC: Dick Cheney, Condoleeza Rice
BCC: Barbara Bush

Hey buddys, yule be mighty pleazed we've found the wmd.

Plz see below...

:)
Dubya x

P>S invade anyhoo.

DYSTOPIAN DAD IN:
A VERY LARGE SOCIAL NETWORKING SITE

DD Hi Sweet Pea! What are you doing there?
Daughter Oh nothing really, just updating my status on *A very large Social Networking Site...*

DD Right...oh I see...
Daughter Daddy? did I do something wrong?

DD Well it's just that *A very large Social Networking Site* looks helpful at keeping us in touch with friends, colleagues, contacts etc. but information is stored in a very large place called the United States.
Daughter OK, but is that bad?

DD Well honey lump, the information is collated into a big repository of facts, stats and personal data - ways to target adverts specifically at you then powerful venture capitalists affiliated with the CIA control that information.
Daughter But surely I can delete things?

DD Past data is stored interminably, so never forgotten. *A very large Social Networking Site* also takes care to collect other data about you from things like blogs, instant messaging services and other users. So like an indelible profile documenting every part of your personal life...
And the best bit is no one's sure quite sure about how the information will be used in the future...
Bless you sweet honey sugar pop!

GREATEST RICK ROLLS IN HISTORY 02

From: Neil Armstrong

To: Mrs Armstrong
CC: Buzz Aldrin
BCC: CIA

Hey Darlin'...we're arrived safe on the moon! It's brilliant up here, really erm mooney, I can see our house and everything...

I've sent a picture here.....keep scrollin'...

Got ya! We're just horsin' around in a studio in some bunker somewhere. I don't even know which state the moon's in anyway. Over.

X Back for meatloaf X

CONSPIRACY THEORIES REVEALED

There's nothing like the scent of government cover up to get the Internet's networks twinkling like area 51's alien air traffic control. Reporter Mal Adjusted gives us a heads-up on the low-down.

Melting Ice Cream

We've all seen it, felt it and tasted it: so-called manufacturers putting a chemical in ice cream that causes the frozen matter to melt over a pre-defined period.
Mal's findings 'I spoke to Carte D'or headquarters and unsurprisingly they didn't want to comment on the exposed revelation. A rather too-convenient case of tight lips and brain freeze, perhaps.'

David Blunkett and Abu Hamza

Never seen in the same place at the same time, now 'both' keeping a low profile.
Mal's findings 'Followed what looked like David Blunkett's dog (cunningly attached to an elderly lady) to a novelty party shop and found him sniffing suspiciously around the captain hook hooks'

Swine Flu

Never seen a pig coughing. Media hysteria in order to smoke screen a wider bacon-based conspiracy.
Mal's findings 'Camped inside inner city farm for two weeks, monitoring pig enclosure – didn't see any pigs coughing, but did notice a morose hen pecking a Benson & Hedges'

My Wife Leaving Me

'Dear John' note on the kitchen table when I returned home from my Elvis in Ilford investigation. Note detailed my apparent 'deranged fantasies'.
Mal's findings 'Unlikely, I had a solid job on a paper that was producing at the time and I know she's been abducted from the secret messages she keeps leaving me in my Cornflakes.'

Next Time

Area 54 – I've long suspected this, we've all heard about Area 51, but what about the more debauched version situated in a New York Studio in the 1980's?

GREATEST RICK ROLLS IN HISTORY 03

From: Rick Astley

To: Mum Astley
CC:
BCC: Legal Dept

Dear Mum,

Please can you stop sending me photos of myself as a young lad. I know you think it's cute but what with all his Rick Rolling business it's really too much to bear. Even the woman at the deli counter said 'Oooh, I've just been rick rolled'. It's terrible. Every time I look in the mirror, it's like a bitter reminder of the public joke and it's like I've been bloody Rick Rolled. Please stop showing the family album to relatives. Or at the very least please scratch my face out of the family snaps with a coin.

Still love you,

Rick

P.S Photo Attached

E-Bay-Gum

The auction site for Northern stereotypes.

Brash Uncompromising Self-Starter
Comes with Mondeo, hands-free headset and a ruddy complexion hewn from overpriced bitter consumption at Travelodges.

Chippy Owner
Overweight, jolly, understands Mushy Peas and likes pouring enough vinegar on your chips to make you cough upon contact.

Scantily Clad Perma-tanned Disco Dolly
In winter attire. Good at staggering through city centres shouting at kebabs.

Coal Shovelling Pit Man
With detachable roll-up, unwashable.

Bread Faced Moaning Pensioner
Has had harder shits than the likes of you.

Wanted! Fight
Local nutbag seeks scrap for your acknowledgement of the existence of Suffolk.

MONEY4NAMINGCLOUDS.COM

Register a domain name now with:
money4namingclouds.com

'I'm Brian, the cloud!'

Why not register your domain name with us? Our business model is simple and effective: we sell the names of things that don't actually exist in reality. The barrel is literally bottomless, we're in cyberspace! Any domain name you can think of, we sell it. It's like naming clouds – hence our name.

The process is simple, you choose a domain name and we'll tell you it's not available. We'll then offer ill-suited alternatives of course and we add all the variants - .co, .com, .std, .vod, .sod, .bod, .eu, .neu, ..., .the lot – infact any initials you can come up with to make your site as insecure to potentially similar cash-in sites as possible – best get them all!

So hurry along and have a look here:

www._____

Can't get that domain name you want? Why not look at our other selection of goodies to name and buy - stars and bits of moon, there's plenty for everyone!

OLIGARCHS

Media centre situated in the nearby Post Office

BUMPKIN MEADOWS FC

Oligarchs! Need to meet that special football club? We have a whole range of British clubs just waiting to take your call - and potentially a large suitcase full of unmarked bills.
Have a look at our hot pitches:

Inauguration 24 April 1704
Capacity Bench currently seats 7 (more with the addition of collapsible patio furniture) Planning permission for 180 thousand seater stadium is pending approval with the Rotary Club.
Record Attendance 23 (Both Teams plus ref); Shankworth under 12's Vs Hamplewick's over 85's 1989.
Address OS REF 2001001
Guided Tours Mondays annually.

Groundsman Tim Blatchford
Background Trees, Ray Trivets' back garden, corn field – with scarecrow.
The quaint English style village is perfect for much needed privacy from the glare of the paparazzi and prying FBI types. The media centre situated in the nearby Post Office is now open up to two days a week (specific days may vary). The local NISA now stocks a wine.

REQUIRED!

Thriving Hub. Perfect for the wags

The guide goat can be hired upon request

ASBO HARRIERS

Inauguration 1965
Capacity 217 – viewed from surrounding housing estates.
Record Attendance 43 – Dogging finals, June 1992
Address Public Rec, Hardbstd, the Pits UR4 IT
Guided Tours Yes. But don't ask SpiderWeb Frank to take you round after 5.30 pm
Groundsman ~~Tommy Trigger~~, ~~Alan Buckfast~~, Bill Axe.
Background This area is truly ripe for development and great for making connections in the local pharmaceutical industry. The ground also has a comprehensive network of CCTV already installed.

McHEBRIDES McNITED

Inauguration 1474
Capacity Fits up to 17 players on pitch
Record Attendance 17 – Hebrides National Finals
Address Rocksedge, Middle Earth, Hebredes
Guided Tours The guide goat can be hired upon request. Official disclaimer is required to be signed prior to boarding.
Groundsman McMcMc.
Background This is a niche club ripe for taking into the 20th century. We welcome new blood – literally – we need new DNA – and our strip is hand crofted. Mchebrides McNited are currently mid-table in the Scottish Premiere League.

CUSTOMERS ALSO BOUGHT

Those Who Bought:

Also Bought:

Those Who Bought:

Also Bought:

Those Who Bought:

Also Bought:

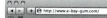

NaivE-bay

Welcome to NaivE-Bay!
Have a look at today's offers!

Kids Bubble Blower
Smells faintly of burnt gas. No clear instructions.

The Animator!
Lethargic children spending too much time in the house and ruining your down time? Well spark some life into 'em with this fully rechargeable mechanised incentive device.

Deal?
NaivE-bay's very own interactive gambling game! This version of Deal or No Deal has Mystery Boxes number one to 480 000 and yours could contain up to 10 thousand pounds. One of them can be yours for the 'Buy it now price' of £78.99. Comes complete with Noel Edmunds: *The Paisley years* action figure.

Blackberry
One half – plus cable – of short-range two-way communication device. Perfect for indoor use and even works around corners (furniture permitting). Bought for £99 a year ago, but on offer for the 'Buy it now price' of £49.99. Compatible with updated Muller Square 'Forest Fruit' model handset.

Children's Modelling Clay
Children's Organic modelling clay. Really let the little 'uns get to grips with nature and increase their immune system in the process with this authentic container of modelling 'clay'. Just add water and away they go!

The Hartley's Collection
The 'Hartley's collection' – a full set of co-ordinated storage solutions. These screw-top ergonomically sympathetic receptacles are perfect for almost anything, especially preserves.

Sands of Time
Your future delivered to you on Etch-a-Sketch. Cannot guarantee messages won't shift during transit.

ELASTIC BROADBAND INC. INTERNAL MEMO

A message from our current CEO and legitimate businessman:

Here at Elastic Broadband we have a long and accountable heritage – going even as far back as 2003 and with only nine major changes to our trading name to date – that's almost less than one per annum.

Profits are up, new secretaries hired, au pairs fired, gardeners handed a small brown envelope of cash for their silence; another year in which to really commit to a productive year and I'm personally going to commit to stakeholder satisfaction by grabbing as much low hanging fruit as possible.

It's been a tough year so I'm told, what with the collapsing economic scenery of the recession, which I'm informed by my legal department to state that we are in no way affiliated to, endorse or were in part responsible for any collapsing scenery nor the recipient of government bail outs. I firmly believe all the initiatives I spearheaded: the customer service structure, for example, will strengthen our market position – whatever that is – and serve the corporations needs beautifully.

It's also sadly tally ho from me :(as I'll be exiting stage left to an exciting new career, somewhere very far from here. Although it may be very difficult to trace or contact me, I'll keep track of dear ol' Lackey Broadband from the comfort of my private jet's window, pressing my nose against the glass, reminiscing about the good old days whilst quaffing Mojitos and changing my name to Carlos.

God bless you all and if any stern-faced men arrive in suits and sunglasses asking for my contact details, please direct them to the Elastic Broadband Customer service number – pressing option 457.
Sincerely,
Charlie Tan

Elastic Broadband CEO & Legitimate Businessman

Farcebook

It's - Ooooh Blimey don't mind if I do Madam - Farcebook!

Share: Status Update

What's on your mind? Fnarrr...

Babs is...holding up a pair of coconuts in front of a market stall

Terry Thomas likes your update.
(21 Hours ago)
K Williams 'Ooooh, I know, bet he liked to update you Babs'
(18 Hours ago)
Babs 'Cheeky, I wasn't after that sort of attention'
(16 Hours ago)
Sid James 'Cor blimey Babs, you've got my attention'
(14 Hours ago)
Babs 'Cheeky beggar! I only wanted to draw attention to those lovely plums behind me'
(14 Hours ago)
Sid James 'Well I've got a banana in my pocket if you want a piece'
(13 Hours ago)
Frankie Howerd 'Can't get into your pictures, Babs'
(10 Hours ago)
K Williams 'It's not your pictures you should be worried about'
(8 Hours ago)
Vicar 'What the blazes is all this rumpus'
(6 Hours ago)
Sid James 'What's the rumpus? Ah now that's a rumpus'
(5 Hours ago)
Babs 'Saucy! Sorry vicar!'
(2 Hours ago)
Vicar 'I'm a man of gawd blimey those look like some ripe fruits'
(1 Hour ago)

R. Asquith is hiding in a wardrobe while an irate husband searches the house
Sid joined the group 'Pwoarr those coconuts aren't shy'
Frankie Howerd's toga's been snagged on a protruding memory stick
Hattie Jaques is berating a randy janitor
R. Asquith Has fallen off a ladder and is hanging from a window ledge

VOUCHERCOD

Offers for all life's little essentials:

These offers are available for the next 10% of the time minus every leap year in the Gregorian calendar.

50% OFF
Half - time orange quarters

15% OFF
'Make your own Sushi kit' comprising of whole un-filleted Salmon

10% OFF
A freight container of Polo mints

87.3% OFF
Semi - colon cleanse and upper - elipsis wax

10% OFF
5% minus 2% plus VAT rise as of 1978 divided by a Bakers dozen and the Ω value.

54% OFF
Full face re-alignment when purchasing leg transplant

23% OFF
18% of left-over Quality Street

50% OFF
The cat's pyjamas, 10% added if purchased with the cat's whiskers

BONUS 72%
Added to all purchases with 28% off or more

10% OFF
Knee-high shagpile carpet

</088/The Web in a Book>

GOOGLE MADE ME VAIN

Tim, 43, from Guilford, Surrey

I'll never forget the feeling I had when I – Tim White - turned up as 14,457,000 in the Google search rankings. I felt lighter than air, barely able to contain myself as I sat in Underworld Lynx Internet Cafe and Money Laundering Facility, spluttering bits of almond croissant across the keyboard and leaving little Technicolor spittle spots on the screen in delight. Previously I had been 15,942,006 and I was getting closer, one blog entry at a time. Still, deep down, I knew some other Tim Whites or indeed permutations of Tim and White were hogging the rankings and I felt the familiar heady concoction of anger and impotence; once again dry – humping the ladder of Internet supremacy.

It wasn't always like this. Innocuously enough it began at work, some colleagues were larking around Googling themselves, seeing whose name came up higher. I tried not to get involved but Derek from accounts had a decent 18043 with his Fly-fishing blog, which had 34 followers. And boy did that smug grin of his point that out.

Some days I would just sit and put my name into a search engine and hit return, pick page 9478 – where my blog proudly sat and click on the thing. If I were to have a wife, I could swear blind she'd have left me, such was my messy compulsion to search again and again and again. And again. And again.

I felt cold, dejected, rejected by an algorithm and always other permutations of my achingly common name – damn you mother! Barry White, White Gloss, White House, hundreds of other Tims, taking up the ranking positions that were my birthright. I cursed to the heavens that my name wasn't something more hit worthy. I've now changed my name to include Barack Obama between Tim and White. The results were astonishing. Still, hopefully this article may help my rankings yet!

Emotional Bay

Emotional Bay - your marketplace to buy and sell emotional artefacts!

Moment of Clarity
Reached whilst cracking heads with fellow wino in park whilst both bending down to reach same can of Tenants Xtra. Still here for sale if you can ask me before midday.

Misspent Youth
Used mainly for daydreaming about winning a reality show, looking in the mirror moaning that I'm not in Heat magazine. Will swap for 2nd round of X – Factor or the buy it now price to be invested in Junior Botox Kit.

Mid-life Crisis
Old enough to know better man undergoing marital difficulties due to fixation with fast cars and inappropriately judged clothing, seeks resolution. Will accept 25 year old blonde, speedboat or being told to 'pack it in Derek' firmly but fairly by spouse.

Suburban Housewife's Hopes
Comes complete with membership to weightwatchers (27 points daily average reached so far), Anne Summers party bookings list, peach basque and unrequited dreams of Mills & Boon.

Invisible Pensioner for Sale
Looks generic, bit ignored.

Left Over Buffet
From ill-attended wedding reception. Comes complete with cheese and petrified pineapple on sticks, Alex Flemming-style coleslaw. Cling-film still partially covering sausage rolls. All food marginally affected by refracted light of a solitary disco ball and a Black Lace echo.

Commuter's Poker Face
Sullen focus on Sudoku and doesn't inflect emotion wrought from years of soul bludgeoning tedium. Low maintenance; only requires ready meal and single serve wine between feet. Comes complete with mobile phone and the phrase 'I'm on the train' emitted upon attachment with poker face.

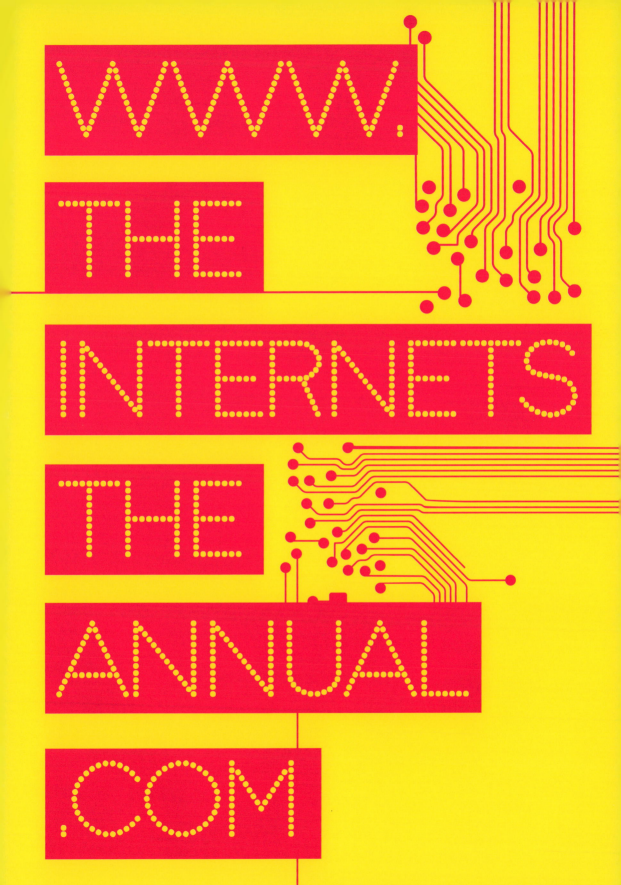

With ex-stock photography model
Ryan Birch

It's me, Ryan Birch! You may know me from various businessey webpages, middle management brochures and any number of brain-buggering Powerpoints. You may even recognise my signature position: the classic brainstorming marker pen pose whilst standing in front of a whiteboard, whilst a chart went upwards, me clenched fist pumping, whilst similarly blandly good looking a good range of ethnically balanced faces smile triumphantly at each other. I use social networking sites like this to keep my hand in. You never know when the next gig's coming from and take it from me – the game is tough! I used to be one of the best stock photography models this side of the M4 corridor – winning Britain's Next Top Stock Photography Model (south east heats) two years running, even becoming the face of Brigshaw toiletries conferences. This little number won't pay my bills forever! That's why I now sell carpets.

GET IN

Priority!
Make sure your photo is tip top – pissing about with angles won't help, if you're not as business-looking as me – use someone else's – perhaps one from my portfolio - for a charge – natch!

Update
Keep up to date with things like social working by updating every seemingly banal breath you take – the punters love it. Latest comments on Ugg boots, the weather, obese children – indeed any old shit seems to suffice and make you look 'on it', as the twitching classes seem to say.

Education
Make this up.

Interests
Don't put yourself – looks vain. Add things that add a dimension – flower arranging or badger sniffing – a talking point.

Groups
Put things charitable – kids and disease things look good.

Connect
Nothing says 'connected' like a large menagerie of contacts, make them up if need be. So far, I'm 11,221 different profiles.

Recommendations
Use one of your own made up contacts and make sure it's saying something businessey and nice. Not about effective methods of getting blood stains out of shagpile. Or tightening the immigration policy.

Also Viewed
Use your made up contacts to check out your profile AND slightly more influential people like the Pope or the classic: Barack Obama.

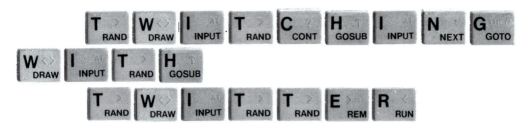

TWITCHING WITH TWITTER

Here's a handy field guide to twitching with Twitter. See if you can spot these types and tick off them all.

The Robin ☐
Magis Taedium
This furtive little fellow is often found re-tweeting the recipe for Jamie Oliver's Moroccan Chicken. Rarely seen and suffers from insecure tweet syndrome fearing attacks from Aquilinus Pedantis.

The Wood Pecker ☐
Non Pertinax
Likes to bang on repeatedly about a subject of personal interest, regardless of reaction. Nests with a like-minded coterie of similarly communicating Peckers. Sometimes forages with Aquilinus Pedantis and can occasionally be found dining on Wikipedia entry corrections in twilight.

The Seagull ☐
Colonia Evacuati
An ungainly beast that flaps over a given tweet, hovers, then evacuates his colon. Can be seen on the Mail Online or tweeting a disparaging remark about the state of the nation on BBC breakfast usually pertaining to the introduction of capital punishment.

The Hawk
Aquilinus Pedantis

A bright display of pedantry lightly covers a substantial lack of actual knowledge on a given subject. A stickler for grammar, punctuation and facts, Aquilinus Pedantis can often seen tweeting self-consciously arch comments from left wing, right-on publications. Cautious to spell check comments on a Word document before the tweet.

The Great Tit
Major Pectoris

Aggressive insistence to fire out a distinctive two syllable or three word tweet pertaining to its surroundings, this rambunctious type joins in with other minor tits roaming and scouring its environment for morsels. Typifies the genus Vacuitus.

The Pink Flamingo
Celebrer Insisto

Likes to nest with a range of celebrity tweeters, in the hope of reflected glory, this gregarious fellow will often be seen adding salacious commentary to the latest celebrity occurrences. Celebrer Insisto has survived mainly on the collapsing scenery of the lives of prat-prone celebrities.

The Parrot
Regurgitati Infinitus

Functioning entirely by re-tweeted findings and seldom chips in with any original comments. Insecure when flying solo Regurgitati Infinitus habitat will often be littered with the remnants of vaguely amusing comedic commentary. Early Stephen Fry lift incident responder.

Illustration: Adrian Dutt

OBSOLETE INCONSEQUENTIALS FROM YOUR PAST REUNITED

Still harbouring suspicions about who wrote 'Giant Bum Boil' on your New Space Hopper? Wonder if that special flame has had the nineteenth sprog by the nineteenth partner and is now 'single'?

Sign In
Forgotten password or changed email address because of the stalking?

Re-unite
Remind yourself exactly why you don't meet up with school mates by attending a school reunion. You'll not only be bored to know they drive a Volvo and have a Golden Retriever, but also see the ravages of time on their haggard faces - smashing any idyllic memories to tiny pieces.

Share
Keep friends up to date with a web of lies and glossy fabrications merely to stymie the boredom of paraphrasing what you've been doing for the past 20 years. (For help with this, please see 'Building your perfect cover story kit' overleaf)

Friendship
Re-establish old pecking orders with a dead arm competition and a game of soggy biscuit. Vow to meet up more often, say in another 25 years time.

Illustration: Adrian Dutt

BUILD YOUR PERFECT COVER STORY KIT

Need help building a life cover story?

Your more interesting identity can be simply assembled by cutting out and arranging the phrases at random.
   Pick one from each section and away you go!

Pick Career
01 Astronaut
02 Dole Scum
03 Pool Shark
04 Brain Surgeon
05 Rocket Scientist
06 Trophy Wife
077 In Recruitment
08 One Armed Trolley Pusher With An Electric Eye

Children's Names
01 Tabatha
02 Wayne
03 Pest
04 Brooklyn
05 Peaches
06 Kylie
07 Chanel
08 Canestan

Where I Met My Partner
01 Thailand
02 Iceland (Shop)
03 Russia
04 From My Work In The Pilchard Factory
05 St Moritz
06 Caravan Park
07 Already Related
08 Park Bench

Vacation Locations
01 Pontins
02 Latvian Ski Resort
03 Hemel Hempstead
04 Hebrides
05 Persian Gulf
06 Ibiza
07 Davos
08 Docks

Activities
01 Heli Gloating
02 Eco Whelk Farming
03 Badger Sniffing
04 Sitting In The Dark
05 Palm Shaving
06 Twitching - Birds
07 Twitching – Curtains
08 Cracking The Ice On My Lake

Further Education
01 Hardknox
02 Marlborough Menthol School For Boys
03 Benson & Hedges Prep
04 Eton Rifles
05 Eckerslike Incomprehensive
06 Vernacular Oratory School
07 Backwater
08 School In The Next Town

Excuses As To Why You Can't Attend Class Reunion
01 Doing Open Heart Surgery That Day
02 Dogs Imploded
03 Pills Haven't Arrived
04 Ran Over Au Pair
05 Signing On
06 Circus Not In Town
07 Reiki Accident
08 Ripped Hole In The Space Time Continuum

Name: Matt Robinson
Occupation: Dole Scum
Next of kin: Chanel
Partner: None. Available
Location: Iceland Shop
Activities: Badger Sniffing
Education: Benson & Hedges Prep

SOCIAL NETWORKING
FRIEND REQUEST LETTER:

Me Cyberspace
You Different Part of Cyberspace

Dear Potential 'Friend'

You've been chosen to validate an aspect of my virtual social identity.

If you'd kindly manoeuvre your virtual representation of yourself into my electronic menagerie by clicking 'ACCEPT', that'd be just great. In all probability your inclusion may make my life look that much better; it may add another dimension to other's perception, or serve to qualify my connection to a past or a social set or allow an insight into my crop cultivation and online farming skills for example.

For the sake of potential social embarrassment overspill into the non-virtual world, please don't just leave me in some holding tank like the 'others'. I'll be here with them in the hope of attaining your virtual approval. During my potentially eternal stay in the infernal limbo I'll be looking onwards and upwards while your cursor of approval hovers over 'accept' or 'ignore' like some hand of god potentially ready to pluck our tormented faces from this weird form of purgatory. I love you. Let's not make this awkward.

■ ACCEPT ■ IGNORE
And face an uncomfortable moment when we meet face to face and possibly a lifetime of unvoiced recriminations.

</100/Ettiquettiweb>

SOCIAL NOTWORKING

The Profile Picture of Dorian Grey:
The visual Diary of an unrequited friend request

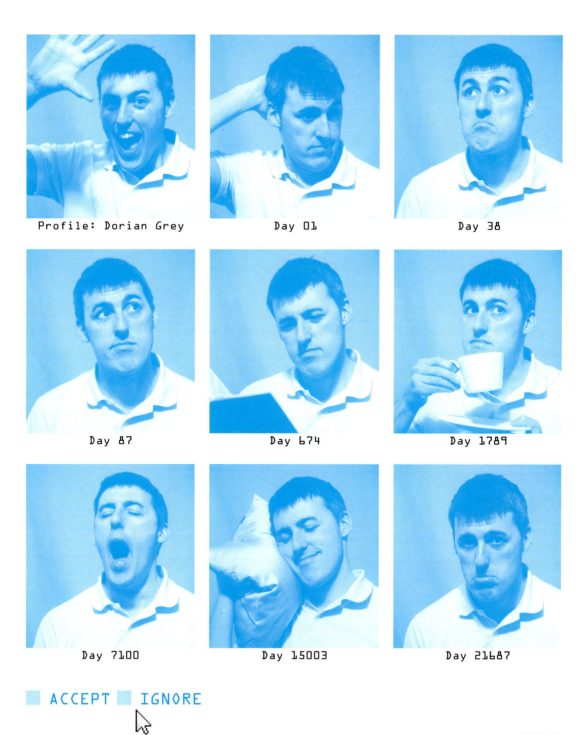

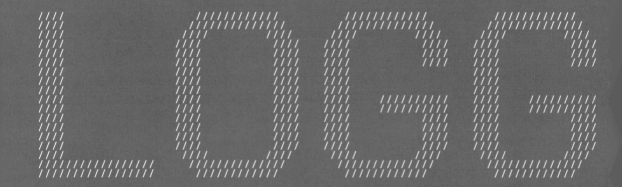

</102/Logging Off>

08

ING OFF

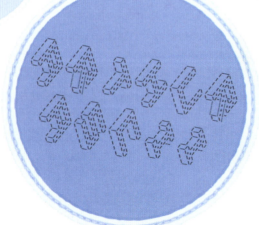

THE

MILLENNIUM BUG PLANNED FOR RE-LAUNCH IN 2012

The society of Skint I.T Consultants would like to point out that a comprehensive overhaul of all Computer Programs, Systems, Software, Hardware, Eveningware, Laptops, Desktops, Croptops, indeed anything with an electronic pulse, must be checked, double-checked by us and then turned off and on again – BEFORE 2012.

We would like to point out that the original millennium bug scare which we were pleased to report reached media hysteria level back in late 1999 was in fact just to test the response and general hysteria level before we really really, honestly do need to check for the previously unknown millennium and three twenty fifth's bug.

Call now on: 0800 LETS PANIC

Everythingistaken.com

Welcome to everythingisstaken.com (formerly Money4namingclouds.com)! We're online live from the Cayman Islands!

We have literally 7 domain names left. Choose from:

www.dkjksjdhkdfjhkdfychinchinoldboy.com
www.cnoaishdoisdhsocheeseandbiscuits.tv
www.mylabialherpes.net
www.brianjenkinsizgayastoast.co.uk
www.967485B.com
www.yahooooooosearch.com
www.wongsdvdshack.org

Bye!

</106/Logging Off>

PAGE LOADING

INTERNET MEME

Inaccurate definitions brought to you by a collection of competing pedants from around the globe.

This article needs additional citations, verification and in all fairness never to see the backlight of a monitor.

Internet Meme (/'mi:m/),
A relatively new term, identifies ideas, beliefs or a trough of sub-cultural horseshit that is transmitted from one person or group of people to another. The concept comes from an analogy: as *genes* transmit biological information, *memes* can be said to transmit idea, belief information, and possibly a catchphrase that will ricochet through the hallways of eternity to the unerring monotonous delight of life forms until the max limit of the memory stick of time.

A meme acts as a unit for carrying cultural ideas, symbols or practices, like poignant epithets of the human condition e.g. the rotund teenage boy wielding a golf ball collector as a Light Sabre, or a baby biting an older brothers finger and said brother expressing said action to the delight of over 200 million easily pleased people. Meme popularity can be transmitted from one mind to another through writing, speech, gestures, rituals or the most popular video sharing platform on the planet, appended with comments and learned assessments leading to modern language development – introducing acronyms like LOL and ROFL or just musings on the semiotics of the phrase 'UR MUMZ A DOUCHBAG'. Supporters of the concept regard memes as cultural analogues to genes, in that they self-replicate, mutate, respond to selective pressures (2) and possibly get their own chat show.

The word meme is a shortening (modeled on gene) of mimeme detritus (from Ancient Greek μίμημα Greek pronunciation *mimēma*, "something im/irr - itated", from μιμεῖσθαι *mimeisthai*, "to im/irr - itate", from μῖμος *mimos* detritus "mind sewage") (3) and it was coined by the British evolutionary biologist (Richard Dawkins) in *The Selfish Gene* (1976) (1) (4) as a concept for discussion of evolutionary principles in explaining the spread of ideas and cultural phenomena. He's no doubt overjoyed that the phrase is now popularly regarded as expressly pertaining to recitals of sociological value like 'Chocolate Rain', or 'It's My Dick in a Box'.

Advocates of the *meme* idea say that memes may evolve by natural selection, in a manner analogous to that of biological evolution. Memes do this through the processes of variation, mutation, competition, and inherttance, each of which influencing a meme's reproductive success - as exemplified in the follow ups of the original international superhighway meme success stories - 'What What in the Butt' particularly benefitting from a subsequent remix.

Memes spread through the behaviors that they generate in their hosts. Memes that propagate less prolifically may become extinct, while others may survive, spread, and (for better or for worse) mutate. Memes which replicate the most effectively spread best. Some memes may replicate effectively even when they prove to be detrimental to the welfare of their hosts. (6) as demonstrated in example a by the rotund star wars teen needing deep counseling after a number of the 21 million people watching said footage decide to point out the lads shortcomings for the rest of his natural life.

This is an evolutionary schema of the phenomenon called Meme:

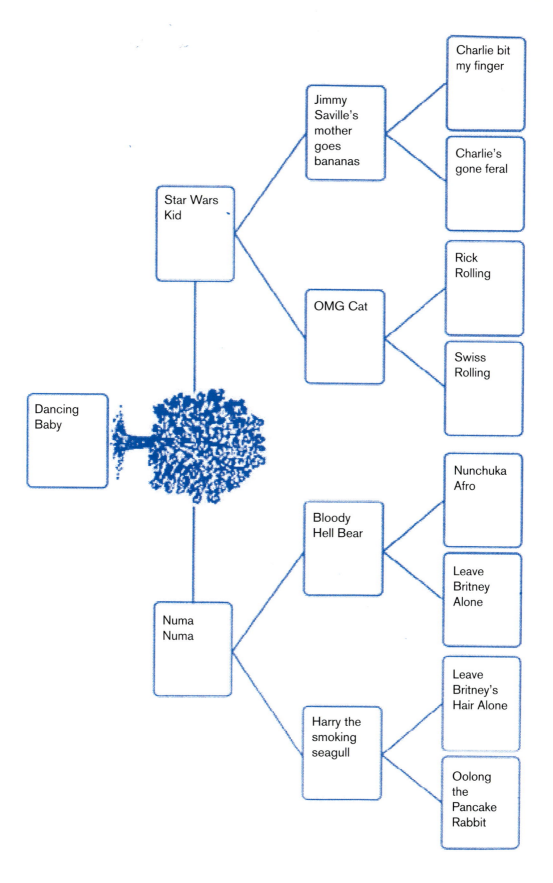

INDEX

A
Advertising 71, 91
African Coup 9
Afterglow, basking in 8
Ailments, Social Networking 34, 35
Amazon 46, 56, 84
Area 51, 78
Arms, Dead 98
Astley, Rick 75, 77, 79
Austin, Jane 56
Austin, Texas 176

B
Bacon 29, 62
Baguette, underarm holding techniques 42
Banjax Cable 62
Barlow, Ken 56
Basque, Peach 90
BBC Breakfast 96
Bennie from Crossroads 46
Birch, Ryan 94
Black Lace (music) 90
Bludgeon, joy 56
Bonus 7, 88
Bonus Point 44,
Bonus, Brucie 54
Book, how to use 7
Book, setting up of 6
Book, this 31, 45, 49, 54
Book, web in a 64-91
Botox, Junior kit 90
Bovine 16, 72
Brain Freeze 78
Broadband, Elastic 26, 27
Bubba, divine meat rod 57

C
Capitalist 9, 76
Carpet 43, 44, 88, 94
Cattle Prod 54, 72
China 29, 31, 32,
Class, Internet Usage by 40
cle'a]n.e y7'r ke]yb29oa;rd 63
Cloud, Word 21

Clouds, Money for naming 81
Clowns, morose 45
Cornflakes 78
Corporations 6, 7
Cover Story, building you 98
Cravat Monthly 40
Crisis, Mid life 90
Customer Service 26, 27

D
Darts, Olympic discipline 42
Davies, Windsor 41
Daytime Sherry 9
Derek, Pack it in, 90
Disclaimer 11
Dog, David Blunkett's 78
Dozen, Bakers 88
DVD 31, 32

E
E-Bay Gum 80
E-bay, and quantum entanglement 13
Eighties (80's) Badges 104
Elastic Snapping 71
Elvis 78
Emoticons 37, 44
Espadrille, Invention of 47
Etiquetiweb, Social 92 – 101
Everything's taken.com 106
Extra, Tennants 90

F
Facebook 28, 29, 74, 76
Factoid 46
Farcebook 87
Farmville 74, 100,
Feet, John Prescott's 69
Filthy Cash in – 11
Freshly Released Killers 57
Frottage 6
Fry, Stephen 12, 97,
Futility 6

G
Geeks 12
Gekko, Gordon 23
Germ Disco's 7, 72,
God, Complex 56
Google 49, 59, 69, 89
Grand Theft Auto 30
Gyroscope 27

H
Hair configuration 13

I
IheartU 62
In, Get 94
India 43
Insouciance, French 42
Interactive 7
Interface 6, 7
Internet and us 38-50
Internet, What is 14-22
Italy 43

J
Japanese Soldiers 7

K
Kaleidoscope 9
Karmic Loops 6
Kerfuffles 16
Kidneys, both of them 27
Kim Jong Ill 9, 47
Kimjongle 47
Klingon 13
KWP 47
Kyle, Jeremy 40, 54

L
L Ron Hubbard 8
Lee, Tim Berners 20, 36, 104
Levitating line 50
Logging in level 12
Logging Off 102
LOL 13
Lucas, George 45

M

Marshall Cavendish 31
McBeal, Alley 8
Mcdonald, Sir Trevor 33
Meme 110, 111
Middle East 29, 43
Middleton, Kate 41,
Mind Spork 6
Moments, created by 37
Moments, killed by 37
Morissey 45
Mother 10
Mothers, little Soldier 10
Mugabe, president 46

N

Need to Know 24-37
Nietzsche, Frederick 56
Nihilist 56
Norden, Dennis 33
North Korea 47
Novice 12

O

Obama, Barrack 95
Oliver, Jamie 40, 96
Onanist 60
Online Gamer 13

P

Pedants 33, 96
Pensioners 12, 45, 90
Pepy's, Samuel 74
Pets 10, 43
Pineapple, Cheese and 44, 58, 90
Polo Mints, Freight Container of 88
Pontly, Pontly and Pontly 8
Poptarts 13
Practical Internet User 52-61
Profile, build your 99
Pumping, Fists 94
Puzzles 62
Pygmy Sniffing 73
Pyjama's, Cats 88

R

Random 28, 31, 99
Randy 62
Reminder Questions 10
Retriever, Golden 98

S

Sarong 73
Scientology 46
Scissors 16, 68
Scissors, conceptual 16
Seagulls 54, 96,
Shake 6
Sir Cliff Richard 16
Skype 28, 29, 49
Slippers, lungs as 57
Spanking, Animals 42
Starbucks 12, 16
Started, Getting 4-12
Stephen Hawking 13
Stereotype, Passing 45
Stevens, Senator Ted 17
Street, Quality, leftover 88
Summers, Anne 90
Suralan 19, 20
Switzerland 43
Sykes, Melanie 44

T

Take a Break 89
Talk Talk 16
Technology 7, 28, 29, 42
Terms and Conditions 8
Thatcher, Margeret 46
Thingaboxem 12
Thingaport 12
Timeline 18
Towelsatdawn 43
Trouble Callers 27
Trouser Press 71
Tubes, series of 17
Tubigrips, grease stains, removing of 40
Twitter 13, 37, 96

U

UK 42, 73
Undergarments 8
Underground bunker 28
Underwear 10, 35

V

Vampire, cynical TV cash in 45
Verification Code 9
Vet Required 45
Viagra, Panda 43
Volvo 98
Vouchercod 88
VSFW 48

W

WAP 22
Webucation 71
Weligeon 71
Wetherspoon's 32, 54, 40
Whichwitch 43
Whiskers, cats 88
Wong 31, 32
Worality 71
www 11, 36, 40, 41, 42, 43, 106

CREDITS

Author: Will Hogan
www.willhogan.co.uk

Art Direction: Transmission
www.thisistransmission.com

Cover Design: Peter Quinell

Illustration: Adrian Dutt
www.adriandutt.co.uk

Creative Juice: Pete Rogers

Publishing Overlord: Emma Barnes
www.snowbooks.com

This book is dedicated with love to Michaela Simova and Oliver Hogan.

My beautiful family, without which I'd have in no way been allowed to indulge myself in these preposterous ramblings -

Heartfelt thanks to the facilitators
The delightful and whip smart Emma Barnes at Snowbooks, Pete Rogers for original ideas (and top grade Tea and Biscuits), Stuart Tolley for his premium skills, nous and patience, Adrian Dutt for shining Illustrative flair. The website of the book is care of the web doyen Conal Wright Newton whose wares can be found here: www.lab-24.com and at www.theinternetstheannual.com

Support, input, love, thanks and general hat doffing supreme to Pat Hogan & Noel Cattermole, Emma Hogan & Marcus Jeffs, Charlie & Jonny, Sarah Cattermole, Joe Cattermole, Dellar's: Agnes, Dick, Harriet, Jonathan, Chris, Laura, Jamie Tott, Sophie Tott, Will & Erin, Matt Robinson, Paul Stirling, Tom Barrow, The Idler, Dan Kieran, Ian Vince, Steven Merchant, Justin Quirk, Paul Mardles, Miles Dunbar, Conal Wright Newton, Justin Wright, Simon Pegg, Tiggle, Trish Stevens, Kate & Moray Hunter, Duncan & Jen Colville, Claire Courtney, Ania Poullain-Majchrzak, Frankie Poullain, Oli Pattenden, James Ward, Dan Holiday, Dan Turner, Stuart White, Alex Smith, Nemone Caldwell, Chukwuji Iwudi, Chris & Melis Maxwell, Dean Beswick, James Lapwood, Emmeline Child, Paul Nolan, Lars Vinther, Steve Walker, Lee Colwith, Tom Haxell, Shintaro Taketani, Stuart Broom, Ronnie Mcbryde, Liz Bannard, Tom Tattersall, Richard Benson, Dominic Grant, Hiromi and Paul Seyb, Claire, Brendan and Leo Smith, Matt Waller & Dave Monk, Rhian Wheeler, Nancy Clarkson, Roy Robinson, Tim Berners Lee, Gavin Matheson, Tim Bryan, Ella Cockbain, Will Peall, Alex Beattie, Nancy Clarkson, Stuart Turnbull, Gary Thornton, Janka, Latsi, Kika, Mamka, Slowka, Otso, all at LWS, Sizewell Beach Cafe, Tony Doyle, Maria Lola Garcia Tejon, Maria Joudina, The Framley Examiner and anyone I've missed out who's made me smile past, present and future.

</112/Logging Off>